Epworth C

Genera
Ivor H

The Epistle to the Colossians

Epworth Commentaries

Already published

The Book of Job
C.S. Rodd

Isaiah 1–39
David Stacey

The Books of Amos and Hosea
Harry Mowvley

The Gospel of John
Kenneth Grayston

The First Epistle to the Corinthians
Nigel Watson

The Second Epistle to the Corinthians
Nigel Watson

The Epistle to the Galatians
John Ziesler

The Epistle to the Philippians
Howard Marshall

The Epistle to the Hebrews
Paul Ellingworth

The Johannine Epistles
William Loader

In preparation

The Gospel of Matthew
Ivor Jones

I and II Thessalonians
Neil Richardson

The Book of Revelation
Christopher Rowland

The Epistle to the
COLOSSIANS

ROY YATES

EPWORTH PRESS

ISBN 0 7162 0492 4

First Published 1993
by Epworth Press
1 Central Buildings Westminster
London SW1H 9NR

Typeset by Regent Typesetting, London
and printed in Great Britain by
Mackays of Chatham

CONTENTS

GENERAL INTRODUCTION

The *Epworth Preacher's Commentaries* that Greville P. Lewis edited so successfully in the 1950s and 1960s having now served their turn, the Epworth Press has commissioned a team of distinguished academics who are also preachers and teachers to create a new series of commentaries that will serve the 1990s and beyond. We have seized the opportunity offered by the publication in 1989 of the Revised English Bible to use this very readable and scholarly version as the basis of our commentaries, and we are grateful to the Oxford and Cambridge University Presses for the requisite licence and for granting our authors pre-publication access. They will nevertheless be free to cite and discuss other translations wherever they think that these will illuminate the original text.

Just as the books that make up the Bible differ in their provenance and purpose, so our authors will necessarily differ in the structure and bearing of their commentaries. But they will all strive to get as close as possible to the intention of the original writers, expounding their texts in the light of the place, time, circumstances, and culture that gave them birth, and showing why each work was received by Jews and Christians into their respective Canons of Holy Scripture. They will seek to make full use of the dramatic advance in biblical scholarship world-wide but at the same time to explain technical terms in the language of the common reader, and to suggest ways in which Scripture can help towards the living of a Christian life today. They will endeavour to produce commentaries that can be used with confidence in ecumenical, multiracial, and multifaith situations, and not by scholars only but by preachers, teachers, students, church members, and anyone who wants to improve his or her understanding of the Bible.

Ivor H. Jones

PREFACE

The epistle to the Colossians holds a special place in the development of early Christian thought, standing as it does half way between the acknowledged Pauline epistles and the undoubted pseudo-Pauline writings of Ephesians and the Pastorals. The exposition of Colossians presented in this commentary is an attempt to look at the epistle in this setting, when the search was on to find new vocabulary to do justice to the experience of Jesus Christ, to express his significance in terms of creation and redemption, and also to apply the insights of the apostle Paul to the changed situation of a later generation.

The approach to Colossians I have pursued here is both critical and devotional. I learned this approach from Barnabas Lindars, who was my teacher for some ten years. Barnabas never shied away from any critical question, but was always ready to follow scholarly enquiry wherever it might lead. At the same time he maintained a deeply devotional approach. I dedicate this commentary to his memory.

ABBREVIATIONS

ABSA	*Annual of the British School at Athens*
BZNW	Beihefte zur *Zeitschrift für die neutestamentliche Wisssnschaft*
CBQ	*Catholic Biblical Quarterly*
EQ	*Evangelical Quarterly*
ET	*Expository Times*
ICC	International Critical Commentary
IDB	*Interpreter's Dictionary of the Bible*
ITQ	*Irish Theological Quarterly*
JBL	*Journal of Biblical Literature*
JSNT	*Journal for the Study of the New Testament*
JSNTS	JSNT supplement series
JSOT	*Journal for the Study of the Old Testament*
JTS	*Journal of Theological Studies*
NICNT	New International Commentary on the New Testament
NovTest	*Novum Testamentum*
NTS	*New Testament Studies*
SBT	Studies in Biblical Theology
SJT	*Scottish Journal of Theology*
TDNT	*Theological Dictionary of the New Testament*
TU	Texte und Untersuchungen zur Geschichte der altchristlichen Literatur
VT	*Vetus Testamentum*
ZNTW	*Zeitschrift für die neutestamentliche Wissenschaft*

Dead Sea Scrolls

lQS	The Rule of the Community or Manual of Discipline
lQpHab.	The Commentary on Habakkuk

INTRODUCTION

(a) The Making of Colossians

The epistle to the Colossians has traditionally been regarded as the reflection of the mature Paul, written during his final imprisonment in Rome and as the pinnacle of development in Pauline theology, especially in the sphere of christology. It is supposed that Colossians was written to meet the challenge of 'false teachers', whose veneration of the principalities and powers compromised the uniqueness of Christ. Slogans and catchwords are taken up from the teaching of the opponents and re-used to present an antidote to error in terms of a high christology (1.15–20), the triumph of Christ (2.13–15), and the high ethical demands of the paraenetic section of the epistle (3.1–4.6). Thus the traditional picture of 'heresy and antidote' emerges. It gives a definite reason for the writing of Colossians, and serves to unite the christology of ch. 1 to the admonitions of ch. 2.

However, this simple picture is complicated by some marked differences in vocabulary, style and theology between Colossians and the undisputed Pauline letters:-

(i) Colossians contains a large number of rare words that do not occur in the genuine Pauline letters.[1] There are thirty-four words which appear nowhere else in the New Testament, and ten common to Colossians and Ephesians alone. Then there are a group of specific Pauline terms which are absent from Colossians, including 'law', 'sin', 'righteousness', 'freedom', and 'promise'

(ii) The style of the letter is marked by a number of peculiar features. There are long and complicated sentences full of verbose expressions, genitival constructions, the piling up of synonymns, and a large number of participles. All this points to a strongly liturgical style and an extensive use of traditional materials.

(iii) In Colossians the Pauline theology has undergone a development which is evident in every section of the letter, and has produced new formulations in christology, soteriology, ecclesiology, eschatology and ethics. As a result of this development many specifically Pauline concepts are omitted.

These differences in vocabulary, style and theology challenge the traditional view of Pauline authorship, and point to a theologian of the Pauline school who composed the letter with the intention of bringing the apostle's word to bear on the situation a generation after Paul's death. In Colossians we have the picture of a church at a point of development later than that of the accepted Pauline epistles, and on its way to the sub-apostolic age. Certainly Colossians is a round peg that cannot be forced into the square hole of the genuine Paulines.

Attempts have been made to account for these differences by suggesting that Paul has borrowed vocabulary and ideas from the Colossian philosophy to present his own high view of the person of Christ. But the differences are so fundamental and deep-rooted as to call for a more radical solution. In recent years there have been two contributions to Colossian studies which have set the study of the epistle in a different direction, one from each side of the Atlantic.

M.D. Hooker[2] has questioned the assumption that Colossians is dealing with a 'false teaching' imposed on them from outside the Christian community. It is simply not true that what the apostle affirms, others have been denying. The strangest feature about the traditional picture of heresy and antidote is the extraordinary calm with which it is met in Colossians. If false teachers did question the uniqueness of Christ by setting him in a hierarchy of powers, then surely their teaching would have been attacked more explicitly and openly. But there is none of the distress which permeates Galatians, no angry outburst such as we find in Philippians, or hint of a problem of rebellion such as we find in the Corinthian correspondence. The teaching of Colossians in ch. 1 is entirely positive, with no suggestion that its christology is developed in opposition to false beliefs in the Colossian church which could in any sense be described as 'heretical' or 'dangerous'. Once the presupposition of 'false teachers' is removed from Colossians the way is opened up for interpreting the epistle in a different and more positive direction.

Hooker's suggestion is a situation in which young Christians found themselves under pressure to conform to the beliefs and practices of their pagan and Jewish neighbours, and that Col. 1.15–20 is an exposition of Christ as the replacement for the Jewish Torah in terms taken from the Wisdom literature. Hooker is right to question the general assumption that the author is dealing with the teaching of opponents in Colossians. But there does seem to be something more than pressure on converts to make use of the Jewish law in order to subdue their former pagan desires and way of life.

The second reappraisal of the Colossian situation has come from F.O. Francis,[3] who in 1975 published a collection of articles dealing with the background of the epistle. He suggests that, rather than providing the occasion for the writing of Colossians, the christology of the epistle represents the common ground between the author and the recipients. Any difference of opinion is seen in terms of an agreed christology. Christology is all-pervasive in Colossians, yet the writer never attacks a view of Christ advocated by opponents. When he does refer to Christ in the polemical passages, Christ is the common ground – the presupposition that makes the argument work. It was perhaps only by presenting his argument in this way that the author could gain a hearing with the Colossians.

Building largely on his exegesis of Col. 2.18, Francis holds that some of the Colossians have been practising a kind of mystical piety and visionary ascent, and leading to the possibility of worshipping with the angels in heaven. He presents a wide range of parallels from the literature of Hellenistic and Jewish ascetic piety, and suggests that the idea of visionary ascent and participation in the angelic liturgy can provide what he calls 'the cultic-ethical nucleus for future model-building'.[4]

The work of Hooker and Francis provides a useful foundation on which to build, as we explore the view that in Colossians we have a church that has moved some way in the direction of the sub-apostolic age. We can then see that the making of Colossians is a response to a situation in which new ideas and vocabulary were being used to express the significance of an emerging Christianity. In language and theology we are on the borderlands between Christianity, Judaism and Gnosticism, and at a stage before self-definition caused each to move in a different direction. Colossians stands at such a cross-roads in the development of early Christianity.

Colossians represents a Christianity which has moved on a generation from that of the accepted Pauline epistles to a situation where the live issues facing the church are no longer concerned with the place of the Jewish law and circumcision for Gentile converts. Instead we witness the search for new vocabulary to express the significance of Christ, and new metaphors to apply the benefits of his death to believers. The imminent expectation of the parousia has gone, there is an idealized view of the apostolic ministry of Paul, and the development of long-term ethics. In the light of these developments the question of why Colossians was written remains to be answered.

It is notoriously difficult to determine what occasioned the writing of Colossians. Like other New Testament letters it takes for granted much that we should like to have been told, and so one has to read between the lines to make an inspired guess at what has been going on. But there is danger then of reading into the text solutions to problems that never existed. The majority of commentators suppose that the author is dealing with some kind of error, and that he quotes slogans and catchwords from their teaching. But what exactly was it? J.J. Gunther[5] lists forty-four different suggestions that have been made by scholars. Over a hundred years ago J.B. Lightfoot[6] identified two elements in the Colossian teaching: one Judaic and the other Gnostic, and attempted to show that both are combined in the teaching of the Essenes. This identification has been superseded by the discovery of actual Gnostic texts at Nag Hammadi in Egypt, and was by no means universally accepted by other scholars at the time. Since Lightfoot opinion has been divided between those who suppose that what we have here in Colossians is some form of Gnosticism, and those who have their doubts about such an identification. But the vast majority are convinced that the author of Colossians was dealing with opponents whose teachings led to a challenge to the uniqueness of Christ, and found a place alongside him for the placation of other spiritual powers. The references which are held to support this view are as follows:-

(a) There are regulations, probably derived from a Jewish source, concerning matters of food and drink, festivals, new moons and sabbaths (2.16). They are urged, 'do not handle this, do not taste that, do not touch the other' (2.21), but the author dismisses these as 'human rules and regulations' (2.22),

(b) There is a pronounced asceticism, 'with its forced piety, its self-mortification, and its severity to the body' (2.23), possibly undertaken to subdue the flesh and induce visions (see 2.18), but which does not lead to a higher moral standard, and is 'of no use at all in combating sensuality' (2.23).

(c) The principalities and powers (1.16, 2.10, 2.15), elements of the world (2.8, 2.20), and angels (2.18) are taken as spiritual powers who were believed to stand between the worshipper and God. Along with Christ they were to be placated and worshipped in order to facilitate the believer's ascent to the heavenly realm.

(d) The pleroma or 'fullness' (1.19, 2.9) is regarded as a technical term for the aggregate of divine powers through which access to God was to be sought.

(e) The author of Colossians refers to this teaching as 'hollow and delusive speculations' (2.8), 'human teaching' (2.8), and 'human rules and regulations' (2.22).

Following the lead given by Hooker and Francis, we have cause to question the traditional interpretation of these references, and of the Colossian situation in terms of heresy and antidote. What then is going on in Colossians? Is there any evidence of a Christian Gnosis here, or is it something more basic where ideas from Jewish, Hellenistic and Christian background meet and cross-fertilize? Is it simply a case of Christians exercising their freedom in Christ, and finding that such freedom got a little out of hand? It is our suggestion that what Colossians is dealing with has its roots in Jewish mysticism rather than pagan philosophical speculation.[7] It would seem that the vast majority of the members of the church addressed by the epistle were Gentiles. Some of these were attracted to certain elements of Jewish mysticism, including the mystical ascent of the initiate to the heavenly realms to witness the angelic worship of God himself.[8] This was known as 'Merkabah mysticism'. The object was to 'see again' the vision of the heavenly court, the throne of God in all its glory, and of the Deity himself vouchsafed to the prophet Ezekiel (Ezek. 1.26). In post-Jamnian times an elaborate system of ascetic practices, coupled with the recitation of hymns and incantations, was developed in order to induce the vision. Although the majority of Merkabah texts come from the fourth century AD and later, it has been shown that these ideas were present at the heart of Rabbinic Judaism, and were linked with the most prominent teachers of the period, including Johanan ben Zakkai. Asia Minor was an area which was strongly influenced by the apocalyptic spirit.[9] Such mysticism formed part of the background out of which Christianity grew in that part of the world.

The rigours of self-discipline, which included legal ordinances, food and drink regulations, and a careful observance of the festival calendar and sabbaths, and which were being commended to the Colossians, were part of the necessary preparation for such mystical ascent. In line with this the 'flesh' seems to them to have meant the lower side of human nature, including the body. By following their detailed regulations they believed they could strip off the fleshy nature and thereby be in a position to receive visions. This stripping off of the flesh is unlikely to have included actual circumcision, but 'circumcision' may have been used as a technical term for the preparatory and initiatory rites. Although attended by great perils, such visionary experience is unlikely to have been condemned, since Paul experienced something similar himself (II Cor. 12.1–10). It is the vaunting of spiritual pride following such visions that is criticized (2.18), and the consequent neglect of soteriology. The further dangers of assimilating teaching from parallel visionary experiences in pagan religion, of the veneration of angels and other intermediaries, and the acceptance of a complete dualism of flesh and spirit, are not yet present in Colossians, but could so easily develop from it. At this stage the principalities and powers are not regarded as evil cosmic powers, but as part of the divine retinue around the heavenly throne (1.16), who are witnessed at worship by the visionary (2.18), and who attended Christ in his triumph on the cross (2.15). The 'elemental spirits' (2.8, 20) refer to the simplistic human tradition represented in the rules and regulations accepted to induce such visionary ascent. This is the raw material out of which Gnosticism developed. We have here what seems like an early stage in a trajectory which leads from the interests of Judaism, through contact with Christianity in a Hellenistic environment, to the later Gnosticism attested in the Nag Hammadi documents which the anti-Gnostic Fathers opposed. It is easy to see how speculation of a Merkabah kind, in itself not objectionable in either Judaism or Christianity, could develop in a different context into the Gnostic concept of the release of the soul from the prison of the body, and how Christ could come to be regarded as only one such agent in the process. This stage has not yet been reached in Colossians. It is wrong to read it back into the Colossian situation, although we recognize that the seeds of this development were already there, soon to germinate in a congenial soil.

The response of the author of Colossians is to draw upon the Pauline tradition, and to apply it to the new situation with which he and his readers are faced. Although there are similarities between the teaching of Colossians and the genuine Pauline epistles, especially Romans, Galatians and Philippians, the probability of direct literary dependence is unlikely.[10] Instead it is suggested that the author was imbued with the ethos of Pauline teaching, and drew on these resources when he wrote. The only secure literary relationship is with the epistle to Philemon. Here the author found a ready-made list of names and greetings (Philemon 23–24), which he adapted, expanded and incorporated into his own letter (4.7–17) to ensure that it would gain a hearing as a message from Paul. Thus he presents a powerful new formulation of Pauline theology in the changed situation that presented itself some time after the apostle's death.

In addition to dependence on Philemon, the author has drawn heavily on traditional materials,[11] hymnic fragments, liturgical phrases, baptismal references, and ethical formulations. He is not the creative thinker that Paul was, but nevertheless has a good eye for the right reference or quotation to suit his case. Also, like Paul, his theology is cross-centred. This was important as the church moved into an age when Docetism became a threat, and Gnosticism was developing. The tendency to over-emphasize the importance of visionary ascent and angelic dignity, and the inflated pride of those who experienced these things, together with the consequent neglect of soteriology and ethics, is what the author addresses himself to. His answer is to quote the Christ-hymn, but in a setting which emphasizes soteriology as well as christology; to stress the believer's identification with the death of Christ in terms of 'stripping off' (the only stripping off required); and to root true Christian experience in practical ethics.

The most likely place of origin for Colossians is the city of Ephesus. It had been the centre of the Pauline mission in Asia Minor, where a number of his letters were written, and the place where the tradition of Pauline teaching was kept alive among his pupils. It is possible that the publication of Colossians, with its use of Philemon, led to the search for and collection of the Pauline epistles. Ephesians, written as the introduction to the newly collected corpus of Pauline letters, draws heavily on the earlier application and restatement of Pauline teaching in Colossians. If this is the case, the author of Colossians played a key role, not only in the restatement of Pauline teaching for his own generation, but also in stimulating the collection and preservation of Paul's own letters.

(b) The Leading Ideas of the Epistles

(i) Christology Christology is all-pervasive in Colossians. In particular the hymn of 1.15–20 presents us with an impressive list of christological titles and ascriptions of priority and eminence, and all applied to one who, within living memory, has been executed by the Romans. It is Jesus of Nazareth who is described as 'the image of the invisible God' (1.15),

as having 'primacy over all creation' (1.15), 'before all things' (1.17), 'the head of the body' (1.18), 'the first to return from the dead' (1.18), and the one in whom 'God in all his fullness chose to dwell' (1.19). C.F.D. Moule[12] suggests that the impetus for describing Jesus with such a wealth of divine attributes was the experience of the resurrection. This led to a search for a new vocabulary to express what had been experienced in Jesus Christ. In the process the significance of Jesus for both creation and redemption was pushed back to the beginning of all things, and pushed forward to the consummation of all things.

It is claimed that the christology of Colossians is an advance on anything in Paul's commonly accepted letters (such as Phil. 2.9–11 or Rom. 8.31–9), particularly the claim that in Christ the entire fullness of deity dwells bodily (2.9), and that 'in him everything in heaven and on earth was created' (1.16). One common explanation for this wealth of christological terms in Colossians is that they were being used, and possibly misused, in the Colossian 'philosophy', and that they were taken up by the author of the epistle to correct their position, and to spell out the real significance of Christ. This, of course, assumes that what occasioned the writing of Colossians was an erroneous view of the person of Christ. But we must beware of assuming that there were opponents at Colossae who held a christology different from that of the author. In fact the author never attacks a view of Christ advocated by the Colossians. Instead a high christology is the presupposition that makes the argument work. The writer continually gives his argument a christological reference in order to engage his readers. Perhaps this was the only way he could gain a hearing from them. Baptismal death with Christ seems to figure largely in the author's reply, and this points not to a neglect of christology but to a need to realize the soteriological and ethical implications of being in Christ.

Although there are parallels to this vocabulary of high christology in Gnostic and Hellenistic writings, the author of Colossians stands firmly within the Old Testament and Jewish tradition. The hymn draws on Jewish Wisdom theology, according to which the Wisdom of God was thought to have been the agent of God's creation. The implication is not so much that Christ was pre-existent as a person and active in creation and redemption, but that the same full presence and activity of God evident in Christ's resurrection and reconciling work was also present at the creation, so that what is pre-existent is not Christ in person, but the power of God that came to be active in him. 'The creation and Christ must be understood in relation to each other: now that Christ has been raised from the dead the power and purpose in creation cannot be fully understood except in terms of Christ, and so too Christ cannot be fully understood except in terms of that wise activity of God which has made the world what it is, which gives the world its meaning, and which will bring the world to its appointed end.'[13]

(ii) Soteriology It is probable that the high christology of the epistle was not in dispute. Rather it is presented as the common ground between the author and the recipients, and is then used as the basis of the author's comments to them. The soteriological setting provided for the hymn of 1.15–20, together with the suggested interpolations, points to the author's underlying interest in the death of Christ. This is taken up in 2.13–15 in a parenthesis on the saving work of Christ. We have here one of the most important New Testament descriptions of what is achieved by the death of Christ, and one of the most emphatic reiterations of the theme of the incorporation of believers in Christ. We are presented with two great metaphors for the death of Christ: the cancellation of the bond (2.14), and the triumphal procession (2.15). The passage is also dominated by the vocabulary of 'putting off' and 'putting on' in dying and rising with Christ.

The vocabulary of 'putting off' is used of the death of Christ and of believers' participation therein (2.11, 15; 3.9). In 2.11 we read the reference to 'circumcision' as a gruesome metaphor for the death of Christ: 'by the stripping away of the old nature, which is Christ's way of circumcision'. It is possible that the Colossians were using the reference to circumcision to denote a release from the flesh to experience visions, aided by ascetic practices and other regulations. The author recalls them to the death of Christ through which alone there is forgiveness of sins. In the light of this in 2.15 we again detect a reference to the death of Christ in terms of a putting off of the body of flesh (see I Cor. 15.53f., II Cor. 5.3f.). 'Putting off' occurs again in 3.9 in the ethical section of the epistle, where believers are exhorted to put off the old way of life and put on the new, to put off vices and to put on virtues.

In each case the vocabulary of 'putting off' denotes a complete putting aside of the flesh. It is used of Christ's death on the cross, of the believer's participation in dying and rising with Christ, and of the ethical implications that follow from being in Christ. The author takes up the language of 'stripping off' and claims that Christ's death itself is the only stripping off required: a once-for-all stripping by which the believer has access to the fullness of God. All Christians share in the death of Christ, as they put off the old way of life and put on the new. Since they have died with Christ they have no need to submit to the regulations and ritual of the philosophy, which with all its talk about dealing with the flesh might give the appearance of wisdom, but in reality is of no value in checking the indulgence of the flesh (2.23). The author stresses that God did not shun the body, but in all his fullness dwelt in Christ bodily. Christ took his body of flesh to the cross. Approach to God is by way of association with and participation in this real death and 'stripping off', and not in any mystical laying aside of the flesh to experience visions or to worship with the angels.

The result of participation in the death of Christ is expressed in Colossians in terms of forgiveness rather than in the forensic categories of justification familiar to us from the Pauline epistles. This represents a view of the relationship of God to man which carries the strongest moral overtones, and points to a background which involved moral behaviour. From the emphasis on the putting off of vices and the putting on of virtues in the paraenetic section of the epistle, and the suggestion in 2.23 that the rules and regulations of the philosophy, for all their severity, might still not be able to contain the indulgence of the flesh, it would seem that the kind of spirituality practised by certain of the Colossians could so easily lead to a neglect of the reality of forgiveness and of the atoning significance of Christ's death. There are similarities with lines of thought which were later to be developed in Gnosticism into a disdain of the flesh and of salvation as a liberation of the real self from the body. The author of Colossians is aware of this direction of thought, and attempts to correct it by emphasizing the moral aspect of the Christian life, the centrality of forgiveness, and the reality of Christ's death.

In the meditation on the work and achievement of Christ presented in 2.13–15 we find two metaphors taken from the background of Gentile secular life used of the death of Christ, namely the cancellation of the bond and the triumphal procession. The preceding verses have been concerned with that fullness or completion which is to be found in union with Christ, and culminating here in the forgiveness and celebration of victory which result from the death of Christ. The whole passage and both metaphors hinge on the cross as the place where mankind's guilt is recorded, the debt cancelled, and the celebration of Christ's victory takes place.

The force of the metaphor of the bond is that it is an autograph written by the accused himself, an IOU which proves him a debtor. It is an acknowledgement that we are under obligation to God because of sin.[14] The debt can only be cancelled at the cross by the divine acceptance of the debt. The sense of obligation in the metaphor of the bond leads the author to consider the voluntary obligation taken on by the Colossians to observe the ascetic rules and dietary regulations associated with the philosophy. These are all superfluous to union with Christ in this death and resurrection, and are represented by the implied 'subscription to the ordinances'. They are blotted out along with the indebtedness caused by sin. The bond is discharged in Christ's death and nailed to the cross.

In 2.15 we have another non-Jewish metaphor exploited in the interests of Christian thinking. The metaphor of triumph has its origin in the spectacular procession and celebration of the Roman triumph. If, as we argue, the central feature of a triumph was not the parade of defeated captives, but the acclamation of the victor and the rejoicing of the people, the emphasis in 2.15 falls on the glorification of Christ following his death, and the celebration of his victory by the hosts of angels, as well as the company of the redeemed.[15] The implication is that there is no room for the élitism of those who practise visionary piety and claim to have ascended to worship with the angels in the presence of God, nor for the suggestion that Christian experience is somehow incomplete without this. The glory of Christ, who is himself the fullness of God, is manifested in his victory on the cross, and is celebrated by all who believe in him. This celebration is shared by the hosts of heaven in public festivity. The metaphor of triumphant celebration is taken up to show that the essence of Christian experience is not just for the few, but for all who are baptized into the death and resurrection of Christ.

Thus the author of Colossians takes up two metaphors from the background of secular life. Each represents a dramatic and arresting picture of the implications of Christ's death and resurrection. In the process of attempting to give adequate expression to Christian belief in the crucified and risen Lord new metaphors were sought, new vocabulary coined, and old words filled with new meaning. The bond and the triumph are among these.

(iii) Ecclesiology There are some marked differences between the Pauline epistles and Colossians in the development of ecclesiology, as well as some points of continuity. The Colossians are referred to as 'God's people at Colossae, our fellow-believers in Christ' (1.2), and the mystery of the gospel as 'now disclosed to God's people' (1.26). The word 'church' continues to be used of the local Christian community, as the author sends greetings 'to Nympha and the congregation that meets at her house' (4.15), and directs that the letter should also be read 'to the church at Laodicea' (4.16). All this represents a continuity with the local reference of 'church' in the Pauline epistles, where Christians are spoken of as the body and limbs of Christ, his very own body (I Cor. 10.16f.;

12.12f.; Rom. 12.4f.). But Colossians comes from a time of transition in ecclesiology when 'church' is not only used in the local sense as in the letters of Paul, but is also beginning to be applied to the wider universal church. Thus in the hymn of 1.15–20 Christ is described as 'the head of the body, the church' (1.18), and it is claimed of the apostle that he completes 'what still remains for Christ to suffer in my own person for the sake of Christ's body, the church' (1.24).

The reference to Christ as 'the head of the body, the church' (1.18) is a new development. It looks like a simplification of Paul's difficulty but creative conception of Christians as the body of Christ. The transference of Wisdom language to Christ may have prompted this development. Also they are to guard against thinking too highly of themselves and of their mystical experience without giving due acknowledgement to Christ as Lord and head (2.18–19). Head is used in 1.18 in its usual sense of 'supremacy'.

In the hymn of 1.15–20 it has been suggested that the original reference was to the body of the cosmos. Christ is the head that governs the body of the cosmos.[16] The cosmos is ruled and held together by his headship. The author reinterprets this cosmological statement by his addition of the phrase 'of the church', which is designated as the place where in the present Christ exercises his rule over the cosmos. 'Church' here obviously has a universal reference. Christ is Lord over the universe, but his body is the church, and is the place where he realizes his world-wide lordship.

In a context where the Colossians were being encouraged to take part in visionary mysticism, the addition of 'the church' would have the effect of rooting the exalted view of Christ, shared by both the author and recipients of the letter, in the historical entity of the church. It would recall the earlier Pauline usage, with its strong local reference and emphasis on being part of the body, and indicate that being a Christian has to do with incorporation into Christ in a concrete setting. Thus the universal and the local reference of 'church' stand side by side in Colossians.

The ecclesiology of Colossians means that the church can be more easily distinguished from Christ than is the case in Paul's genuine letters. This has bearing on the interpretation of 1.24, where the author has no hesitation in claiming that what is lacking in Christ's suffering is filled up by Paul in his body on behalf of the church, which is Christ's body. He did not mean to imply that Christ's sufferings were in any way deficient,[17] but that the hardships Paul endures in the course of his apostolic ministry are for the sake of the Colossians and the whole church. It is in his unique capacity as apostle-minister that Paul, in suffering and in preaching, fulfils the office God has given to him to make known the mystery of the gospel (1.25–26). This idealized view of Paul and of his apostolic ministry cannot have been written by Paul himself, but comes from the hand of a disciple. It presents a view of ministry and of apostleship that stands half-way between the genuine letters and the Pastorals.

In ecclesiology and in his view of ministry the author of Colossians has taken up these ideas from Paul's thought and developed them to fit the circumstances of the next generation. The disciple has taken a step beyond the master, but in the process he has lost some of Paul's eschatological tension.

(iv) Eschatology Eschatology in Colossians has receded into the background, and the expectation that the Lord would soon come has disappeared. Instead of awaiting his coming they are exhorted to make the most of the time (4.5), and are presented with longer-term ethics (3.1–4.6) than we find in Paul. There is a different way of looking at the world and at the Christian life in terms of a present enjoyment of the fruits of the coming age that would be more appropriate to a later generation. Hope has become part of the content of the gospel message to be preached throughout the world (1.5, 23, 27), and faith has become objectified as 'the faith that is believed in' (1.4, 23; 2.7).

This difference of emphasis has its effect on the view of baptism in Colossians, which is presented in terms of dying and rising with Christ (2.12, 3.1). Note the contrast with Rom. 6.4, where Paul says that in baptism Christians have died to sin and live by faith in the resurrected Lord. The resurrection of believers is regarded as an event in the future still to be experienced. But Colossians speaks not only of the fact that they have died and been buried with Christ in baptism, but adds, 'you have been raised with him'. The resurrection to new life is regarded as having already taken place, and is described by means of an aorist tense in the original Greek. REB translates it 'you were raised'. Life with Christ is now the present reality. What is still to come in the future is the revelation of that life which was received in baptism, and is now hidden with Christ in God (3.3). Colossians repeatedly uses the phrase 'with Christ' in a context where death and resurrection with Christ has already taken place in baptism (2.13, 20; 3.1, 3). It is a formulaic phrase which takes on almost the same meaning as 'in Christ' and describes the appropriation of the new life received in baptism.

The fading hope of an imminent parousia, the shift in terminology, and the hint that resurrection is already realized in baptism are important reasons why Colossians cannot be Pauline. Ephesians carries this tendency a stage further to depict believers as actually seated in the heavenly places (Eph.2.6), while in the Pastoral Epistles the author complains of those who teach that the resurrection has already taken place (II Tim.2.18). Again Colossians can be seen to stand at a point of transition in the development of ideas and the use of vocabulary.

(v) Ethics The fading hope of an imminent parousia, with the adoption of a realized eschatology, has its effect on the paraenetic section of Colossians. We witness the development of long-term ethics, with an emphasis on appropriate standards of behaviour for Christians living in a pagan environment. The contrast with the lack of specific ethical commands in Paul's letters is marked, and especially evident in Galatians, where Paul is content to exhort them to walk by the Spirit and to let faith work itself out in love. Here in Colossians we find traditional lists of vices and virtues, together with the household code, padded out with suitable proverbial sayings, to form a block of moral instruction and exhortation which takes up almost one third of the epistle. Much of this ethical material has antecedents in Jewish and Hellenistic moral instruction,[18] but is used here in its distinctively Christian form for the first time.

This points to a situation where the moral and ethical outworkings of being a Christian were being neglected. The Christian way of life presented here is meant to be an effective counter to those who would neglect the reality of Christ's death for the more glamorous interest in 'visionary experience'. Christian life needs to be rooted in the reality of Christ's death. It is also the basis of Christian ethics. The view presented is also a reflection of a church that has moved on a generation from the ethics of Paul, and is more content to spell out what is required of Christians living in a pagan environment in terms of specific guide-lines and rules. The controversy over the place of the Jewish law which prevented Paul from doing so is a thing of the past. The creative tension between Spirit, faith and love is lost, although the distinctive Pauline emphasis of the Christian way of life following from association with the death of Christ is retained.

It will be seen from this survey of the leading ideas of the epistle that many of the matters normally dealt with in Introduction are irrelevant to our exposition of Colossians, such as descriptions of the city of Colossae and its environs, or speculation about where the apostle Paul might have been imprisoned. However, the following suggestions might aid our understanding of the text:-

Authorship It is not possible to decide with any certainty who wrote the epistle. The selection of names from the personnel mentioned in the greetings of the letter is not helpful. At best all we can say is that the author was acquainted with the Pauline tradition, and wrote in the apostle's name to bring Paul's word to his own generation. He may have belonged to a Pauline school in Ephesus.

Date Again there is no certainty beyond the fact that the author wrote for a situation that had changed from that which confronted Paul. A date in the 80s is probable.

Place of Writing Ephesus is the most likely place. Indeed the epistle might have more to say to the situation of the Christian community in Ephesus than to the churches of the Lycus Valley. The fact that the city of Colossae was destroyed by an earthquake in AD 61[19] need not affect the question of authorship if we can contend with the possibility that Colossae was already destroyed at the time when the letter was written, and was known to be so.[20] This underlines the fact that its message is relevant to more than one community, and that its main thrust could have been to the writer's own community, possibly in Ephesus where the Pauline school was based.

(c) The Relationship with Philemon

Philemon is the shortest letter in the Pauline corpus, and the only one addressed to an individual. All the rest are addressed to church communities either founded by Paul or about to be visited by him. The occasion of the letter is that Philemon's slave, Onesimus, had run away and had taken up refuge with Paul. Paul was in prison at the time, probably in Ephesus. Having embraced the Christian faith Onesimus had been able to render useful service to Paul. But Paul could not keep him, and had no authority to do so. Onesimus was therefore sent back to his master with the letter to Philemon.

It is to be noted that Paul does not demand anything in this letter. Although he had every right to use his apostolic authority, Paul refrains from doing so, and leaves the outcome entirely to Philemon.[21] In contrast to Pliny's letter pleading for a runaway servant,[22] Paul says nothing about repentance on the part of the slave, and there is no explicit appeal for forgiveness on the part of the master. The terms we should expect such a letter to contain are conspicuous by their absence. Instead it is made clear that Philemon's obligation is to receive back Onesimus as a Christian brother (v.16). Paul asks, 'welcome him as you would welcome me' (v.17). If freedom is granted to Onesimus it is to be without obligation and in fulfilment of the love commandment. Paul gives his personal guarantee in writing, a commitment that would have been legally binding, that if necessary he would defray any expenses himself (v.19). There is also a play on the name Onesimus, which means 'useful'. Paul claims that before his conversion he was 'once so useless to you, but now useful indeed, both to you and to me' (v.11).

The letter is addressed not just to Philemon, but also mentions Apphia, Archippus, and the entire church community in the opening greeting (v.2). This makes Philemon something more than a private letter. The whole church community is made aware of the apostle's word in order to ensure that on his return Onesimus is received into their fellowship and sustained by love.

The outcome of Onesimus's meeting with his master Philemon, and his reception in the church community, is not known. However, when passing through Asia Minor at the beginning of the second century AD on his way to his martyrdom in Rome, Ignatius of Antioch greets the Bishop of Ephesus by the name of Onesimus.[23] It is not unreasonable to suppose that this is the same Onesimus in whom Paul saw so much promise.

The letter to Philemon was included in the Pauline corpus from the beginning. It was not the kind of letter that would have been added subsequently. Why should Philemon have been included when it is so unlike the others? J. Knox[24] suggests that some personal consideration must be held to account for the incorporation among the Pauline letters of this personal note. Philemon was an important document for at least one person – Onesimus. Could he have been one of the persons responsible for the collection and publication of the corpus of Pauline letters in the last decade of the first century? Knox believes that this link explains the presence of Philemon in the collection, and further that it provides a convincing motive for the creation of the collection. There are close connections between Philemon and Colossians. Philemon is undisputably an authentic Pauline letter. However, there is a growing body of opinion among scholars that Colossians is a pseudo-Pauline letter. If this is the case the author of Colossians would have taken up the names of personnel mentioned in Philemon, along with other ideas, to help authenticate his own letter, as he attempts to apply the insights of

Pauline theology to the situation of his own church in the 80s. There are several points of contact, some of which can best be explained in terms of literary dependence.

(1) In Philemon 5 Paul says he has heard of Philemon's love and faith. In Col. 1.4 the author says the same thing using practically the same words. In both cases the love and faith of the addressees are the grounds for and immediately follow the mention of the author's thanking God for them in prayer. But Col.1.4 straightens out the grammar of Philemon 5, and makes it clear that faith is properly directed towards the saints.

(2) The cheirograph in Col. 2.14, a bond of obligation whose cancellation is used as a metaphor of forgiveness, is a figure which may have been suggested by Paul's having given his word of bond in Philemon 19.

(3) In Col. 3.11 the author points out that in Christ there is neither slave nor freeman, but Christ is all in all. This is followed in 3.12 by the exhortation to put on, among other things, 'compassion' or 'tenderness of heart'. Part of the phrase appears three times in Philemon (vv. 7, 12, 20), indicating the attitude that Paul expects of Philemon in his dealings with Onesimus.

(4) The appearance of the *Haustafel* in its fully developed form in Col. 3.18–4.1, and with its lengthy treatment of master-slave relations, is a natural development from Philemon. There is obviously a concern to avoid encouraging disloyalty in slaves, but the reciprocal obligations of masters is also stressed.

(5) Onesimus is presented by Paul as a co-worker in Philemon 13, and he also appears as a co-worker in Col. 4.9.

(6) The list of Paul's co-workers overlaps to a large degree, although the names are not in the same sequence. Both Philemon 1 and Col. 1.1 name Timothy as co-operating with Paul in sending the epistle. The names found in Philemon 23f. recur without exception in Col. 4.10–14, although in a different sequence, and all with added details except Demas.

If Colossians was composed by a disciple of Paul he must have known and used Philemon, not only to provide an epistolary introduction and conclusion, with suitable Pauline personnel, but also to provide inspiration for some of the leading ideas of the epistle.

COMMENTARY

Preface and greetings
1.1–2

Most letters, whether ancient or modern, are written communications addressed to those from whom the sender is separated by distance. The letter is therefore a substitute for the personal presence of the sender and for the communication of direct speech. In Hellenistic and Roman times there was already a well-established tradition of letter-writing. Etiquette demanded that the letter began with the names of the sender and the recipients, together with customary greetings and benedictions.[1] In spite of being such an unlikely vehicle to convey instructions or doctrine, the letter became the most popular literary form in early Christianity. This was because letter-writing had become an established part of the Pauline missionary strategy, as a means of keeping in touch with congregations founded either by the apostle or by one of his associates. The letter, often delivered by one of his associates, was a substitute for Paul's personal presence. In the letters he often dealt with issues about which we have little other information, and in which so much is taken for granted as understood between writer and recipients, that the exegete has to read between the lines and make an intelligent guess at what has been going on. In spite of these difficulties it is through the epistles that we are given a window through which to view the internal life of the early Christian communities.

The Pauline preface follows the oriental model for a letter, but the details are filled out in a distinctively Christian way, so as to transpose the traditional introduction and letter form into a new genre. There had been nothing quite like the Christian epistle previously. When the first generation of Christians leaders died, others of their school continued to write in the guise of and with the authority of their masters. Colossians is an example of such a pseudepigraphical writing. The opening lines are taken word for word from II Cor. 1.1, and are themselves repeated with only minor additions in Eph. 1.1f. The author takes up the name of his mentor, the apostle Paul, coupled up with Paul's close associate, Timothy, to convey greetings to the Christian community at Colossae, and to authenticate the message he has to deliver. A similar function is performed by the mention of a number of Paul's other associates in the list of greetings in 4.7–17.

It is now no longer an accepted practice to write a letter or other work in the name of someone else, even though a number of modern authors write under a pseudonymn. However, in ancient times it was quite common for a pupil to write under the name of his master, both to honour him, and to bring his word to a wider readership.

1.1 Colossians opens with the name of *Paul,* the name the apostle used in the Hellenistic-Roman world instead of the Jewish name of Saul. He introduces himself to a Christian congregation not known personally to him, and which was founded by Epaphras, one of his colleagues (1.7). But his relationship to the Colossians is set out in the title *apostle of Christ Jesus*. Paul writes not as a private individual, but as one commissioned by the Lord himself to preach the gospel to the Gentiles (cf. Gal. 1.1, 15–16). There is some confusion in the New Testament about the use of the title 'apostle'.[2] It appears to be a fluid term, used sometimes in a general sense of one who is sent as a messenger (cf. John 13.16; II Cor. 8.23); sometimes in a technical and restricted sense of the Twelve (cf. Luke 6.13; Acts 1.26): and yet again in a technical sense which includes others in addition to the Twelve, such as Barnabas and Paul (Acts 14.14). The apostle formed the highest rank of ministers in the early church (cf. I Cor. 12.28). Paul's claim to be among their number was challenged in Galatia and at Corinth (Gal. 12–20; I Cor. 9.1–3; II Cor. 10–13). By the time Colossians was written the heat and tension of those days was past, and Paul is presented as the apostle *par excellence*, unrivalled and without mention of any other apostle. There is therefore no need to mention the title again after the opening verse. Paul's apostleship is *by the will of God*, in that it is a direct gift from God, and not conferred through others (Gal. 1.12).

Alongside Paul is *Timothy*, his helper and co-worker. Timothy is also mentioned in the preface of II Corinthians, Philippians, I and II Thessalonians and Philemon. According to the Acts of the Apostles Timothy was a native of Lystra, the son of a Jewish mother and a Greek father. He became a Christian during the first visit of Paul and Barnabas to his home town. He later joined Paul as his associate. Paul circumcised him to regularize his anomalous religious status (Acts 16.1–3). He held an esteemed position among Paul's helpers, as the warm tribute paid to him in Phil. 2.19–24 shows. However, after the mention of Timothy in the opening verse of Colossians, he is not mentioned again in the letter. This makes one suspect that his name is being used, alongside that of Paul, to authenticate the author's message as a word from the apostle. He is in no sense co-author of the letter, but stands alongside others mentioned later in the letter as *our colleague*.

1.2 The author now turns to describe the recipients of the letter, *to God's people at Colossae, our fellow-believers in Christ*.[3] Note that the word 'church' does not appear here, as it does in the letters to Thessalonica, Corinth and Galatia. In common with Romans, Philippians and Ephesians, the Colossians are designated as *fellow-believers*. They are the holy, dedicated people whom God has chosen for himself. The Colossian brethren are also called *faithful*, in the sense of 'believing', i.e. Christian, rather than 'trustworthy' (as in 4.7, 9). This further strengthens the idea of Christians as the real Israel. They become God's own people by being incorporated *in Christ*.

The Colossians are wished *grace* and *peace*. The former is God's unconditional goodwill towards men and women expressed in the saving work of Christ, and the latter 'well-being' in the widest sense of the word, and which follows from receiving the divine grace. All this comes *from God our Father*. This is the only one of the Pauline letters in which the name of Christ is not joined to that of God in the opening greeting. But too much should not be read into this, since the author proceeds to a description of Christ in more exalted terms than in any of the earlier Pauline epistles.

Thanksgiving
1.3–8

The second main section of Colossians is the introductory thanksgiving paragraph. Such a thanksgiving is to be found in every extant Pauline letter, except Galatians, I Timothy and Titus. The author follows the customary Hellenistic epistolary model, where thanks was often expressed to the gods for good fortune bestowed. The form is Hellenistic, but the content of the Pauline thanksgiving is based on Old Testament and Jewish thought. This is not a devotional interlude, divorced from the main emphasis of the letter, but is used to form the theological basis of what is to be said later.[1]

The author has received encouraging reports from his associates, who inform him that the Colossian church is making steady progress in faith and brotherly love. The latest report from Epaphras, the founder of the church there, confirms what he has heard before. He therefore prays for their further progress.

It is difficult to follow the line of argument in 1.3–8. It takes the form of a single, overloaded sentence, replete with participial phrases and genitival expressions.[2]

Thanksgiving is the essence of all Christian worship, prayer and praise. It sets the worshipper in the proper relationship to God the Creator and giver of all good things. There is special cause for thanksgiving when someone is received into the faith and shows the signs of belonging to Christ in the fruits of spiritual growth.

1.3 The thanksgiving is expressed in the plural *we thank him for you* (as I Thess. 1.2; 2.13; 3.9: II Thess. 1.3; 2.13). Is this a epistolary plural, 'I thank . . .' or a real plural, 'Timothy and I thank . . .'[3] Paul often oscillates between 'I' and 'we' with no apparent change of meaning. Even when he uses the plural it is still Paul the individual who is speaking, but with a consciousness of apostolic authority.

The prayer of thanks is offered *to God the Father of our Lord Jesus Christ*. The form of words here is quite exceptional. Elsewhere we find, 'the God and Father of the Lord . . .' (Rom. 15.6; II Cor. 1.3; 11.13; Eph. 1.3; I Peter 1.3). The phrase has obviously been shaped by the confession of God as the Father and of Jesus Christ as Lord (cf.

II Cor. 11.31), possibly in a liturgical context. The translation, 'God, who is the Father . . .' seems best.[4] Such thanksgiving is made by the apostle every time he says his prayers. *All* or 'always' here means regularly at the time of prayer, rather than unceasing thanksgiving.

1.4f. The occasion for the thankful prayer derives from the good reports received about the Colossian community from Epaphras (1.8), and is summed up in the familiar Christian triad of *faith, hope* and *love*. These three were probably part of pre-Pauline catechetical teaching (Rom. 5.1–5; I Cor. 13.13; Gal. 5.5f.; Eph. 4.2–5; I Thess. 1.3; 5.8; Heb. 6.10–12; 10.22–24; I Peter 1.3–8, 21f.; Barnabas 1.4; 11.8; Polycarp, Phil. 3.2–3). A.M. Hunter[5] suggests that they were part of a compendium of the Christian life current in the early apostolic church, and possibly inspired by a saying of Jesus. Here in Colossians each quality is further defined. *Faith* here is the sphere rather than the object of faith. It is a reference to their life 'in Christ' rather than to Christ as the one in whom they have believed. Such faith proves its reality by working through *love*. *Hope* is not the subjective attitude of expectation, but the thing hoped for, – the objective treasure *stored up . . . in heaven*. Why is there this concrete meaning of hope in Colossians? Some have suggested it was a caution against false teachers who were trying to rob them of this aspect of the Christian message, possibly by denying any future dimension of Christian salvation. But it could also be a caution to those who assumed that all had been given in their visionary experiences. Such a hope they *previously heard* when the gospel was first preached to them at Colossae, and the church founded. *The true gospel* (cf. Gal. 2.5, 14) is a reference to that preaching.

1.6 Several features of the gospel are now set forth. First it made its triumphal progress, coming to the Colossians, and taking up a place in their lives, since it *came to you*. Also its progress at Colossae was at one with its dynamic spread *the whole world over*. At first sight this might seem like a wild exaggeration, but bear in mind Paul's missionary strategy of establishing Christian communities in all the major cities as centres from which the gospel could spread into the surrounding areas (cf. Rom. 15.23). The true gospel proclaims its truth by its universality, in contrast to the local idiosyncrasies of false gospels. The spread of the gospel is described by the participles *bearing fruit and making new growth* which are reminiscent of Gen. 1.22, 'be fruitful and multiply', and of the parable of the sower in

Mark 4.8, where the seed that fell into good soil 'brought forth grain, growing up and increasing'. W.L. Knox[6] maintains that the phrase is a Gnostic catch-word from the teaching the author is attacking, but this is by no means certain. The writer's train of thought now moves back from the world-wide aspect of the gospel's progress to the beginnings of the Colossian church, *as it does among you*. The true gospel, as taught by Epaphras, was an offer of free grace, *God's grace*, as compared with a code of human devising.

1.7f. The Colossians *were taught* the gospel from Epaphras. Usually Paul describes the acceptance of the gospel as 'believing', 'hearing' or 'obeying', rather than 'learning'. The verb 'to learn' is found only infrequently in Paul.[7] Is it used here to endorse the ministry of Epaphras over against the teaching of the philosophy to emphasize the fact that he gave them systematic instruction?

Epaphras is mentioned again in 4.12 and in Philemon 23. The name is a shortened form of Epaphroditus. One of Paul's fellow-workers appears under that name in Phil. 2.25 and 4.18, but there is no reason to identify the two. In Philemon 23 he is described as Paul's fellow-captive, but we know nothing of the circumstances in which he earned this description. As a native of Colossae (cf. 4.12 'one of you') he had been the evangelist of the Lycus valley, where there were now flourishing churches in Hierapolis and Laodicea, as well as in Colossae.

The descriptions used of Epaphras not only express the apostle's confidence in him, but also state that he is Paul's representative in Colossae. He is described here as *our dear fellow-servant*, and in 4.12 as 'a servant of Christ Jesus'. He is also described as a *trusted worker* or 'minister of Christ'. The term 'minister' originally denoted one who performed service of the lowest kind,[8] but is used by Paul as a title of honour for his closest associates. E.E. Ellis[9] even suggests that 'ministers' were a special class of co-workers active in preaching and teaching (I Thess. 3.2; I Tim. 4.6; Col. 4.7; Eph. 6.21). Epaphras ministers on Paul's behalf, so the Colossians can be sure that he has faithfully conveyed the truth of the gospel to them.

The variant reading here 'on *our/your* behalf' is one of a series where there is confusion about whether the reference is to the first or second person. J.L. Houlden[10] suggests the uncertainty may be due to the practice of dictating manuscripts to a number of scribes in a scriptorium, where words that sounded alike could easily be mistaken.

The Spirit. There is practically nothing in Colossians about the Holy Spirit, although the genuine Pauline letters abound in such allusions. Where Paul speaks of the Spirit's presence with believers as the guarantee of thelr resurrection and eternal inheritance (cf. Rom. 8.11, 15–17), this letter speaks of the indwelling of Christ as the hope of glory (1.27). Was there a danger that Spirit-language would be misrepresented at Colossae, perhaps because of their interest in angels?

Intercession
1.9–14

The author passes from thanksgiving to intercession. It is in this prayer that the main themes of the epistle are previewed. The recipients are to be filled with knowledge of the divine will in wisdom and spiritual perception. All this is to work itself out in practical terms, in appropriate behaviour. They are to bear fruit in all their activity. The author's claim is to present everyone mature in Christ. The passage does not have an obvious climax, but passes almost imperceptibly from the form of a prayer to that of a hymn.

1.12–14 uses traditional baptismal language, recognizable by the 'participle' style, and the appearance of a series of terms not otherwise used in Colossians or in the Pauline corpus. The author refers to the transfer from one authority to another, from the power of darkness to the power of light. The metaphor here refers not to a future eschatological hope, but to the present condition of life in Christ. In him they have their liberation, which is identified as 'forgiveness of sins'. The phrase is absent from Paul, and is uncommon in the New Testament. Reference to the 'redemption' wrought by Christ makes the transition to the christological statements developed in the hymn of 1.15–20. 1.12–14 can be seen as an introduction to the hymn, a sort of introit, setting the hymn in a context of redemption, rather than in abstract speculation.[1]

The object of prayer of intercession is not to ask God to intervene and affect the material course of events, nor to request him to transcend the laws of his creation, but rather that those prayed for might know that they are held up before God, that they are cared for and supported. Great comfort and strength can be derived from this knowledge. Here the prayer is that the Colossians might grow to the fullness of spiritual development, meet with fortitude whatever comes their way, and be able to look forward to sharing in the final inheritance of God's people in Christ. All this is made possible by an acknowledgement of the lordship of Christ and the forgiveness of sins.

1.9 The author's prayer is that God might fill the Colossian Christians with a perception of his will, which consists in an understanding of what is spiritually important. Notice how the terms used, *full insight, wisdom, spiritual understanding,* have links with the world of speculative ideas which developed into the Gnostic religion. But in this context they are rooted in practical ethics and the outworkings of the Christian gospel. *Knowledge* here is not the secret insight into an esoteric system available only to a few privileged initiates, but insight into God's will. As such it has its roots in the Old Testament and in Jewish thought,[2] and is concerned with right conduct. 'Wisdom' and 'insight' are also characterized by this practical orientation, and are thus opposed to a speculative view of wisdom. The adjective *spiritual* is notoriously difficult to interpret. E.G. Selwyn[3] paraphrases the text here; 'sanctified by the Spirit and influenced by grace'.

1.10f. This correct understanding is to show itself in the fulfilment of the right conduct of life. The author characterizes the life and behaviour of the Christian by the verb 'to walk', and in this he is indebted to Jewish tradition. The traditional Jewish basis to this prayer is given a Christian orientation by the addition of the words *worthy of the Lord*.

In secular Greek *pleasing* usually signifies an ingratiating desire to gain favour, but it could also be used in a positive sense, as it often was in Hellenistic Judaism, to refer to what was 'well pleasing to God'.

More Jewish expressions are taken up in 1.11. In order to be able to maintain this conduct worthy of the Lord the community is to be strengthened and filled with the power of God (cf. Eph. 1. 19f.). *Fortitude and patience* are the signs of the loyal Christian.

1.12 Here the Father is praised because he has effected salvation and redemption for his people in Christ. The whole section is full of Old Testament echoes. *To share the heritage of God's people* recalls the promise made to Abraham, and renewed to Israel, that they would enter and possess the promised land as their inheritance. Although the manuscript evidence is again evenly divided between 'you' and 'us', the parallel in Eph. 1.18 and 2.19 favours the former, as Paul the apostle is portrayed as addressing his Gentile readers. *Inheritance* or 'what is allotted' refers to the portion of the promised land given to Israel. As God's people in the Old Testament received their apportioned lot in the promised land, so God's people in the New Testament receive their lot in the Kingdom of Christ, the realm of light.

It is possible to take *God's people in the realm of light* as a reference to the angels (cf. 1QS vi,7–8),[4] and to hold that the writer is countering any desire to join the angels (or to venerate them) by insisting that Christians have already attained a place shared by the angels. But it is more likely that what is referred to is membership of God's chosen people.

1.13f. Using traditional material, which some commentators claim to be of baptismal origin,[5] the author refers to the transfer of people from one authority to another, from darkness to the realm of Christ. There are strong associations with Exodus imagery here, particularly in reference to being *rescued* and *brought into* God's *kingdom*. Light and darkness are universally used as symbols of truth and falsehood, good and evil. *The domain of darkness* is a reference to their former way of life, and not to the personified powers of evil. The claims of Christ now take priority since they have come under the 'lordship' of Christ, *the kingdom of his dear son*. This constitutes one of the few references in the New Testament to the 'kingdom of Christ'. Paul's view is best seen in I Cor. 15.24–28, where it appears that Christ will hand over his rule to the Father when all his enemies have been brought into subjection. The dominion of Christ, into which the faithful have been transferred, mediates salvation to them here and now. Participation in this salvation is expressed by the use of the first person, 'us' and 'we', and has the result that *our release is secured* and *our sins forgiven*.

In its secular usage redemption has to do with the release of captives from imprisonment, bondage or slavery.[6] But in the New Testament usage, the emphasis is on deliverance rather than on the payment of a price.[7] This again recalls the deliverance of Israel from captivity in Egypt by the power of God, and without the payment of a ransom price. The suggestion of David Hill[8] that the word could be interpreted in terms of the atoning and propiatory deaths of the martyrs, rather than the ritual of the Day of Atonement, adds further emphasis to the meaning of deliverance and liberation.

In v.14 redemption is virtually equated with the forgiveness of sins. The phrase has no parallel in the rest of Paul. For Paul sin is usually seen as a quasi-personal force from whose rule Christ has brought deliverance. Only in I Cor. 15.3 does he come near to the idea of our present passage. The shift from a dramatic view of Christ's death to forgiveness, with its strong moral overtones, was probably part of the author's programme to counter the idea that it was possible to be initiated into a higher spiritual state, available only to an esoteric minority. His concern was to show that the benefits of Christ's death are available to all believers.

These verses contain traditional terms and imagery, taken from the context of baptismal theology (cf. Rom. 6.1–4; Col. 2.13), and set out the implications of the salvation wrought by God in Christ. Along with 1.20–23, they form the setting for the following Christ hymn of 1.15–20, firmly clamping the christological and speculative statements of the hymn in a theology of the death of Christ.

Hymn: The Lordship of Christ in Creation and Redemption

The Great Christology: An Early Christian Confession

1.15–20

Anyone who writes on Colossians must come to terms with this difficult and crucial passage. More has been written about these verses than any other passage in the epistle.

THE STRUCTURE AND ORIGIN OF THE HYMN

Peculiarities of style, language and theology identify 1.15–20 as traditional material, set out in the form of an early Christian hymn or confession. There is a rhythmical lilt, and a correspondence between words and phrases, which suggests a rudimentary metre and facilitates an arrangement of the words into verse form. There is also an unusual vocabulary. The verses contain an impressive number of terms which either do not appear at all elsewhere in the Pauline corpus, or are used with a different meaning. All this suggests that we are dealing with a primitive liturgical statement in the style of a confession or creed. The form is not that of either Hebrew or Greek poetry, but the rhythmical prose found often in early Christian hymnody.

The pioneer in recognizing a structured hymn in these verses was E. Norden.[1] He found in them 'undoubtedly primitive traditional material', which he considered came originally from Jewish circles influenced by Greek ideas. He divided Col. 1.12–20 into three verses: 12–14 being a liturgical introduction, 15–18a dealing with Christ and creation, and 18b–20 with Christ and the church.

Since Norden's time a number of scholars have attempted to set out the passage in verse form, but with varying degrees of success. E. Lohmeyer[2] arranged 13–20 in a pattern of 3+7+3+7 lines, and suggested a background in the theology of the Jewish Day of Atonement. E. Käsemann[3] considers that we are dealing with a pre-

Christian hymn to a Gnostic redeemer, adapted for Christian use as a baptismal liturgy by a number of interpolations. He suggests that the passage divides into two verses, 15–16 and 18b–20, which were connected by 17–18a. J.M. Robinson[4] has attempted to produce a hymn of two verses of matching symmetry, but only at the cost of deleting certain words from the text and rearranging others. He then constructs a proposed 'original' draft of the hymn, which the author of Colossians supplemented and reinterpreted to serve his purpose. E. Bammel[5] contends that the hymn consists of two verses, each containing an elaborate chiastic parallelism. In the search for hymnic perfection one writer has even suggested a tune to which his reconstructed hymn could be sung, with 17–18a acting as a refrain or chorus.[6] The consensus of scholarly opinion seems to be that this is a pre-Pauline hymn to Christ, interpolated by the author of Colossians at v.18 by the addition of *the church*, and at v.20 by the addition of *through the shedding of his blood on the cross*. But there is always the salutary warning issued by C.F.D. Moule[7] that many of the arguments based on rhythm, parallelism and supposed arrangement into verses are precarious enough at the best of times, and most of all when there is no recognizable quantitative metre by which to judge. Certainly the danger of making unhelpful amendments to the text in order to fit the hymn into a predetermined structure is to be avoided.

Despite such reservations there is obviously a liturgical foundation to Col. 1.15–20. The arrangement into verses is indicated by the repetition of key words and phrases. There appear to be two verses, 15–16 and 18b–20, with 17–18a acting as a transitional link between them. The suggestion has been made by P. Benoit[8] that only the first verse, celebrating the role of Christ as creative Wisdom, circulated independently before incorporation into the letter, and that the second verse was constructed on the model of the first. Certainly it is curious that in the twenty-sixth edition of the Nestle-Aland Greek Testament 15–18a are set out as poetry, and 18b–20 as prose.

The text as we have it could conceivably have passed through at least three stages of development:

(a) a pre-Christian hymn in praise of Wisdom (15–16);

(b) the composition of a matching verse celebrating the role of Christ in redemption (18b–20), along with a transitional link (17–18a) claiming for Christ that which is ascribed to Wisdom in the first verse;

(c) at least two interpolations by the author of Colossians (*the church* in 18, and *through the shedding of his blood on the cross* in

20), as well as a liturgical introduction to the hymn in 12–14. All this is conjecture, but it does help to make sense of this difficult and yet crucial passage for the understanding of the letter.

There is also a wide divergence of opinion concerning the background to the hymn. In proposing a Gnostic background Käsemann[9] notes that by removing the words *the church* and *through the shedding of his blood on the cross*, every Christian motif would be eliminated. Furthermore, when 15–20 are contrasted with the litugical, joyful, eschatological emphasis of 12–14, the metaphysical drama of the Gnostic redeemer stands out. He therefore traces the source of the passage to a pre-Christian hymn based on the Gnostic myth of the archetypal man who is also the redeemer. But, apart from the question of whether a Gnostic redeemer myth existed at the time Colossians was written, Käsemann's view does not take into account the obvious Old Testament background of many of the terms and concepts of the hymn.

C.F. Burney[10] does take the Jewish background of the hymn seriously, setting it in the context of Jewish Wisdom speculation. Judaism had already ascribed to Wisdom a precosmic origin, and a part in the creation of the world. He tries to show how Rabbinic speculation about the word *reshith* in Prov. 8.22 and *b'reshith* in Gen. 1.1 has links with the 'firstborn of all creation' in Col. 1.15. The twofold role of Wisdom in creation and redemption is applied by the author of Colossians to Christ. W.D. Davies[11] takes Burney's interpretation a step further by suggesting that the application of Wisdom terminology to Christ was made by Paul (whom he takes to be the author of Colossians), because of his concept of Christ as a new Torah who replaces the old. The Torah in Judaism had already become identified with the Wisdom of God, and given the qualities of pre-existence and participation in the creation of the universe, as well as the redemption of mankind. Davies thinks that the occasion which compelled Paul to develop his early equation of Christ with the Wisdom of God (I Cor. 1.24) was the Colossian philosophy.

Burney's line of reasoning is complicated, but his search for a background to the hymn in Jewish Wisdom speculation is on the right lines. R.P. Martin[12] refers to 'an emerging consensus' that the hymn relates to a Gnosticizing trend within Hellenistic Judaism, mediated through the Phrygian synagogues, and picking up ideas which are found in Wisdom literature. What started out as an attempt to give some expression to the immanence of God and his continued involvement with creation, in a Hellenistic environment was also related to parallel concepts in pagan philosophy and the mystery religions. In Jewish theology, against a background of monotheism, Wisdom invariably remained a personification of divine action and will. But without the constraints of monotheism the way was opened for the development of these concepts in terms of an independent divine being. We are at a point where Judaism, paganism and Christianity were dealing with similar terminology, but proceeding to develop the ideas along different lines. J.D.G. Dunn[13] says, 'The first Christians were ransacking the vocabulary available to them in order that they might express as fully as possible the significance of Jesus.' The personified Wisdom was a way of speaking of God's activity in creation and redemption. In Col. 1.15–20 this is applied to Jesus Christ, who only a generation previously had been put to death by crucifixion.

THE INTRODUCTION AND APPLICATION OF THE HYMN

The use made of the hymn by the author of Colossians, who provides a liturgical introduction (1.12–14) and a practical application (1.21–23), in addition to interpolations to the actual hymn, underlines his concern with the theology of atonement. Col. 1.12–14 draws on traditional material, and by the use of the first personal pronoun *us*, applies the theology of the hymn to the Colossians. The setting is that of the salvation, wrought by God in Christ, which consists in the fact that *our release is secured and our sins are forgiven* (1.14). The writer is concerned to show that the benefits of Christ's death are available to all believers, and not just to an esoteric minority.

The author of Colossians continues to expound his theology of atonement in 1.21–23, as he presents a kind of commentary on the hymn which interprets and applies the cosmic work of Christ to the readers. The reconciliation, which in the hymn has a cosmic dimension, is here rooted firmly in the experience of the believer and in the life of the Christian community. The alienation referred to in 1.21 has been limited by some commentators to refer only to the Gentiles. This is certainly how Eph. 2.12 interprets it, transposing the meaning of reconciliation so that one of its major factors becomes the unity of Jew and Gentile in Christ. But here the alienation is that which is caused by sin. Such reconciliation is presented as an already accomplished fact for believers, whereas the cosmic reconciliation of *all things* in the hymn still awaits completion. In Christ the Colossians already have all the benefits of Christ's death – something which even the angels of heaven have yet to experience. *His body of flesh and blood* is added to demonstrate that reconciliation is accomplished only at the cost of a true incarnation and of Christ's physical suffering. The church is the body of Christ because Christ has died for them. It is not possible to belong to the exalted body of the Lord without being baptized into his death.

THE THEOLOGY OF THE HYMN

When read in the light of the author's introduction and application, with their stress on atonement, the place of the hymn in the argument of the epistle takes on a different complexion. The author of the epistle grounds the speculative theology of a cosmic christology in the life of the church and in the death of Jesus on the cross. It has even been suggested, and with some justification, that the exalted christology of 1.15–20 was not the point at issue between the author and the readers. F.O. Francis[14] holds that 'The pre-eminence of Christ over all powers was the presupposition held in common by writer, reader and errorists. Traditions such as 1.15–19, 2.9, 2.10b and 3.1c were not at issue. The argument lay in their soteriological and eschatological implications.' There were those at Colossae who did not realize the full implications of the fact that in Christ, and through his death on the cross, they were reconciled to God, they were forgiven, they had died and been raised with Christ, and their salvation was complete. Instead of accepting the fact of their redemption, they still struggled to subdue the body, to be released from the flesh, and so to enter the heavenly realms. Christ was their pattern in throwing off the flesh, but they failed to realize that it was in the very real world of flesh and blood that their redemption had been wrought.

The first verse of the hymn (15–16) celebrates the role of Christ in creation. It shows signs of being a pre-Christian Wisdom hymn. In the context of contemporary Judaism, with its stress on the transcendence of God, the problem was of how God could be known. The language of personification, applied to the Word and Wisdom of God, the Torah and the Angel of the Lord, helped to overcome this obstacle. Thus personified Wisdom was a way of speaking of God's activity in creation. The twofold role of Wisdom in creation and redemption is applied by the author of the hymn to Christ.

On the face of it the hymn proclaims the pre-existence of Christ, who as a person was active in both creation and redemption. But J.A. Ziesler[15] advises us that our knowledge of Wisdom language should make us cautious in drawing this conclusion. It is possible that what is meant is that the same full presence and activity of God evident in Christ's resurrection and reconciling work was also present at the creation, so that what is pre-existent is not Christ in person, but the power of God that came to be active in him. Thus the first verse of the hymn can be read in terms of what the Colossians and the author of the epistle have in common, namely a desire to ascribe to the exalted Christ the same purpose of God which was present in creation. The vocabulary of angelic dignity adds to that glory.

1.17–18a forms a transitional link between the two main verses of the hymn. The cosmological perspective of the first verse is taken up in the assertion that Christ is *before all things*, and that *all things are held together in him*. But the thought passes to a soteriological perspective by the author's emendation to the hymn. In its original form it is suggested that 18a read, *He is the head of the body*, and that this was a reference to Christ as the head of the body of the universe. The addition of *the church* would then have the effect of transposing this cosmological and mythical statement into an ecclesiological one. The concept of *body* is defined by *the church*, and thereby understood as an historical entity. It would also correct an implied notion that the world was physically the body of Christ, and permeated by him in a crudely literal sense. Furthermore, if there were people at Colossae who claimed to be a part of Christ's glorified body because of their esoteric experiences, the addition of *the church* would recall the original sense of *body* in the Pauline epistles, with its soteriological associations and close link with the local community. This soteriological emphasis leads on to the final verse.

The final verse of the hymn (1.18b–20) takes up the terminology of the first verse, celebrating the role of Christ in creation, and develops its Wisdom theology to celebrate the role of Christ in the new creation, especially with regard to the work of reconciliation. The parallelism between the two verses has led to the suggestion that the second was constructed on the model of the first. Each begins with a relative clause, followed by two predicates of Christ, and develops his relationship to *all things*, one in terms of creation and the other in terms of reconciliation.

The hymn reaches its climax in the affirmation that *in him God in all his fullness chose to dwell*, and *all things* are reconciled through him. This is almost the same as saying that God was pleased to dwell in him (2.9). It has been claimed that *fullness* is a technical term taken over from Gnosticism for the totality of aeons emanating from God. But according to Valentinian teaching, the pleroma is the heavenly fullness to which God does not belong. Hence this understanding of the word cannot contribute anything to the explanation of 1.19, where God himself is called the pleroma. It is a mistake to try to read such ideas back into the New Testament. The more likely background for the phrase *all his fullness* is the Old Testament, which recognizes that God himself (or his glory) fills the whole universe (Jer. 23.23); and Wisdom literature, where Wisdom is conceived as pervading all things (Wisd. 7.24). It gives the sense that 'Christ is thought of as containing, representing all that God is; and that the destiny of Christians, as the Body of Christ, is to enter, in him, into that wealth of completeness'.[16]

The consequence of this indwelling of God's fullness is described as the reconciliation of the universe. Although there is no previous mention of it, the presupposition is that the unity and harmony of the cosmos have suffered dislocation, and require reconciliation. Reconciliation properly relates to persons. How then can it be applied to the universe? In II Cor. 5.19 Paul seems to be implying that reconciliation has a wider application than believers only. Rom. 8.19–23 too suggests that the whole of the subhuman creation has been subject to the frustration of not being able to fulfil the purpose of its existence until the redemption of mankind has been accomplished. The universe is reconciled in that heaven and earth have been brought back to their fulfilment in the redemption that Christ has brought for all who are incorporated into his death and resurrection. According to the author of Colossians, this has been brought about, not in some other-worldly drama, but through something done in history, through the death of Christ on the cross.

No part of the cosmos is outside the compass of the divine reconciling work. The second proposed emendation to the hymn, the addition of *through the shedding of his blood on the cross* to 1.20, has the effect of transforming the meaning of reconciliation. The cosmic theology of the hymn proclaimed a universal harmony because of the Creator's work in Christ. It seems that the author of the epistle wanted to relate this more closely to Christ's death on the cross, thereby insisting that redemption comes, not by knowing the secrets of the universe, not by indulging in speculation, but by the forgiveness of sins. This ties up with the setting which the author has provided for the hymn in 1.13f., with its emphasis on forgiveness, and in the application of the theme of reconciliation to the Colossians in 1.21f. It also shows that the cosmological statements in the first part of the hymn are to be understood in the light of the soteriological statements of the second verse.

Our suggestion is that a form of the hymn was known and used by the Colossians. From it they derived some support for their view that Christ was exalted above all things among the angels who guard the presence of God. They too desired to throw off the encumbrance of the flesh to ascend to the divine presence. They did not question the christology presented in the hymn, but failed to realize the soteriological implications of their desire for such esoteric experiences. By a series of interpolations, and by setting the hymn in a context of forgiveness of sins, and with a direct application to the readers, the author of the epistle shows that Christ's work is firmly grounded in the church, not amidst the heavenly powers, and in the giving of his life on the cross. It is for all who are in Christ, not just a privileged few.

Thus the hymn celebrates the lordship of Christ in creation and redemption. It contains a wealth of new vocabulary and categories to express the significance of Jesus Christ. At this stage of development in Christian thinking there was a search for new vocabulary as the church moved out from exclusively Jewish circles in the Gentile world. The person of Christ is first set out in relation to creation, as the experience of Christ as lord is expressed in relation to the beginning of all things in creation. Jesus of Nazareth is now the cosmic Christ, as language which in Jewish circles would be thought appropriate only for God is used of him. In the second part of the hymn the exalted terminology of the first verse is earthed in terms of redemption, his lordship of the church, and the reality of his death on the cross. The glories of heaven and the realities of earth are combined in Jesus Christ. There is instruction here for those who preach, in that theological exploration and exposition needs to be earthed in everyday life and experience. When the two are combined they result in a powerful force for mission and apologetics.

1.15 It is widely accepted that 1.15–20 is a pre-Pauline hymn, to which the author of Colossians has added at least two explanatory phrases, and reinterpreted by using it in a soteriological setting. In its present context in Colossians the hymn relates Christ to both creation and redemption. Most would also agree that the hymn can best be read in two verses, with a connecting link. Both of the main verses begin in the original Greek text with a relative clause, translated in the REB *He is* (literally 'who is'), and they are followed by a number of designations of eminence and superiority which relate Christ to the work of creation and of redemption. Many of the terms used are peculiar to Colossians in the New Testament, or are used elsewhere only with a different meaning. All this points to a liturgical origin for this passage.

The hymn begins in praise of Christ by asserting that he, the beloved Son, is *the image of the invisible God*. Although this recalls the story of creation in Genesis 1, and the making of man in the image of God (Gen. 1.26f.), the reference does not adequately explain the phrase in Col. 1.15. Nor is the key to its meaning to be found in the Platonism of Greek philosophy, or in Gnosticism. The closest parallel comes from the Old Testament and Rabbinic theology, where the figure of Wisdom is accorded a pre-cosmic origin and a part in the creation of the world. In a strictly monotheistic religion, such as Judaism, one of the problems was concerned with how a transcendent God could be known. Personified Wisdom was found to be a useful way of speaking about God's activity in creation. Thus, in the Wisdom of Solomon 7.25f., the presence of God through his Wisdom is described:

> Like a fine mist she rises from the power of God,
> a clear effluence from the glory of the Almighty;
> so nothing defiled can enter into her by stealth.
> She is the radiance that streams from everlasting light,
> the flawless mirror of the active power of God
> and the image of his goodness.

'Radiance', 'mirror', 'glory', and 'image' come close to what is said in II Cor. 3.18–4.6. and Heb. 1.3, and to what is developed in Col. 1.15f. As Wisdom is the image of God, so also is Christ:. The great difference between Jewish Wisdom speculation and what we have in the New Testament is that we are dealing with the man, Jesus of Nazareth, and not an abstract concept.

The first title of majesty is closely followed by a second, *primacy over all creation* or 'firstborn of all creation' These words have become among the most disputed and commented on in the whole of the New Testament. Was the intention to describe Christ as a creature, the first created being, or to describe Christ's sovereignty over all creation? It all depends on whether the genitive is read as an objective genitive ('over all creation'), or as a genitive of comparison ('before all created things').[17] The former indicates a primacy of status, the latter a temporal priority. Since the Arian controversy of the fourth century AD there has been a tendency to regard the two as mutually exclusive. But there is a similar ambivalence in Jewish Wisdom theology, where Wisdom is spoken of as both created by God (Prov. 8.22; Sir. 1.4; 29.4), and as the agency through which God created (Prov. 3.19, Wisd. 8.4–6).[18] The important thing about personified Wisdom was that it was a way of speaking of God's creative activity. For the Christian the reference here is to the resurrected and exalted Lord, the pattern of the new humanity, and he who represents the purpose of God for humanity and all creation. The power of God revealed in Christ is the same power which God expressed in creating all things. In this sense Christ is both prior to and supreme over all creation.

1.16 The statement about the unique position of Christ now receives further definition – *because in him everything in heaven and on earth was created*. The use of the passive form 'was created' signifies that God is the Creator (the aorist tense is used at the beginning of the verse, the perfect tense at the end). We are still in the realm of Wisdom theology, through which the author of the hymn is saying that Christ is the creative power of God; he is the means by which God made the world. But is it the intention of the writer to ascribe pre-existence to Christ, as many commentators have supposed? The language here may be used to indicate the continuity between God's creative power and Christ without the implication being intended that Christ himself was active in creation.[19] Nevertheless in Colossians we are at a point of transition in the application of exalted terms to Christ. When we move from the personified Wisdom of Jewish theology to the application of this language to Jesus Christ the next stage on this trajectory is to ascribe pre-existence to him.

Thrones, sovereignties, authorities and powers are included in the created beings who are related to Christ in this way. They are summed up in the inclusive phrase *all things, the whole universe*,[20] of which *in heaven and on earth* is a further explanation.

What are the *thrones, sovereignties, authorities, and powers*? It would seem that they are spiritual powers or angelic beings, but are evil as well as good spirits included, demons as well as angels? Furthermore, although the primary reference is to spiritual powers, does the list include earthly dignities as well?

(i) The primary reference is to the host of God, the angels of his presence, mentioned to establish his majesty and power.[21] They are part of the totality of creation.

(ii) The possibility that the list includes both good and evil powers[22] appeals especially to those who suppose the existence of a Colossian heresy, where worshippers were being encouraged to placate the 'powers' alongside Christ. But if this is the case, why does the author not condemn such a tendency in more overt terms?

(iii) The reference to 'authorities' in Rom. 13.1–7, and to 'the rulers of this age' in I Cor. 2.8 has led some commentators to suppose that the cosmic powers stood behind and operated through the current political powers and religious interests.[23] There is no hint of this view in Colossians.

The first of these three options is preferable. There is certainly an interest in angelic powers in Colossians, almost to the point where soteriology and ethics have been neglected. But the inclusion of powers of evil in the list of 1.16 has been challenged by W. Carr.[24] He begins with the absence of lexical evidence for interpreting the 'principalities, powers and authorities' as hostile spirit powers before the second century AD. Although Judaism exhibited a growing interest in angelology, evil was focussed in the figure of Satan[25] and the demons. Carr concludes that there was not the material to hand in the Jewish background from which such a mythological view of the principalities and powers could be constructed at the time, and that such a view only came to the fore under the influence of Origen at the beginning of the third century AD.

Turning to Colossians Carr[26] begins with 1.16, where he holds that there is no reference to malevolent powers, but only to the unseen heavenly powers, mentioned elsewhere to establish God's majesty and power. They add to the majesty of Christ as Lord (cf. 2.10). The interpretation of Col. 2.15 in terms of a parade of defeated captives in triumphal procession is also challenged. Instead we have a picture of Christ leading his triumphal armies and celebratory hosts. They are the same heavenly host mentioned in 1.16 and 2.10. Christ was instrumental in their creation, they have always been his, and now they adore him after his struggle in the public celebration of his splendour. The cosmic powers that have often been assumed to dominate the lives of the Colossians are in fact not mentioned in the letter. This throws into question the whole notion of a cosmic background to Paul's thought, according to Carr. Although he might have overstated his case, it has at least been made clear that one can no longer assume that the references in Colossians to principalities and powers are to the cosmic powers of evil.

The first verse of the hymn (1.15–16) can be read in terms of what the Colossians and the author of the epistle have in common, namely a desire to ascribe to the exalted Christ the same purpose of God which was present in creation. The vocabulary of angelic dignity adds to that glory.

1.17 The affirmations of 1.15–16 are recapitulated in the twofold affirmation that *he exists before all things and all things are held together in him*. Christ so fully represents and reveals the divine purpose and Wisdom that only the language of eternity can do him justice. He is the sustainer of the universe and the unifying principle of its life.

1.18 Col. 1.17–18a forms a transitional link between the two main verses and passes to a soteriological perspective, which is maintained until the end of the hymn. In its original form it suggested that 1.18a should read *he is the head of the body*; a reference to Christ as head of the body of the universe. *Head* here carries its usual meaning of supremacy.[27] The idea that the universe can be compared to a body is well attested in ancient times.[28] It is proposed that the words *the church* were added as a gloss to the hymn, probably by the writer of Colossians. This would have the effect of transposing the cosmological and mythical statement into an ecclesiological one, so that the concept of *body* is defined by *the church*, and thereby understood as an historical entity. It would also correct an implied notion that the world was physically the body of Christ and permeated by him in a crudely literal sense. The thought of the cosmic Christ holding the universe together is a staggering one, but is this what the text means in Col. 1.18?

In the original hymn it is likely that *body* referred to the cosmos. The reference to '*body*' would call to mind Paul's use of 'body' in the earlier epistles. The obvious link is with Paul's description of Christians as 'the body of Christ' (I Cor. 10.16f., 12.12, 27; Rom. 12.5). This earlier identification is 'overwhelmingly impressive, and theologically of the greatest importance'.[29] Being part of the body of Christ is a parallel to being 'in Christ'. Believers are baptized into his body, where they participate in his death and resurrection, and become part of the new humanity. Why then should the author of Colossians narrow down the scope of the reference by the addition of *the church*? If there were people at Colossae who claimed to be a part of Christ's glorified body because of their esoteric experiences, the addition of the church would recall the original sense of 'body' in the Pauline epistles, with its soteriological associations and close link with the local community. It is usually claimed that *church* in Colossians is used in a universal sense of the whole church, but we are in fact at a stage of transition. It has a clear local reference in 4.15f., while in 1.18 and 1.24 the writer seems still to have the local community strongly in view as well as the universal reference. The universal reference is developed in Ephesians (1.22; 3.10; 5.22–32).

The final verse of the hymn (1.18b–20) takes up the terminology of the first verse, celebrating the role of Christ in creation, and directs its Wisdom theology to celebrate the role of Christ in the new creation, especially with regard to the work of reconciliation. The parallelism between the two verses has led to the suggestion that the second was constructed on the model of the first. Each begins with a relative clause, followed by two predicates of Christ, and develops his relationship to *'all things'*, one in terms of creation and the other in terms of reconciliation. The primacy of Christ is expressed in the terms *origin* and the *first to return from the dead*. It is because of the resurrection that he is the founder of a new humanity, the new creation. In virtue of this it becomes clear that 'his is the primacy over all creation' (1.15) and he is *to become in all things supreme*. Christ's death and resurrection are the source of new life to others, the means by which they are incorporated into the life of the church. But this is only the beginning of a unity which is to embrace the whole universe.

1.19 The hymn reaches its climax in the affirmation: *For in him God in all his fullness chose to dwell*. A minor exegetical problem is concerned with the subject of the verb. 'God' could be supplied as the subject, with the sense 'God was pleased to dwell in him'. Certainly God is the subject of the reconciliation in the next verse. But it is also gramatically possible to regard 'all the fullness' as the subject. This is almost the same as saying that God was pleased to dwell in him.

It has been claimed that 'fullness' or 'pleroma' is a technical term taken over from Gnosticism. Certainly it was used in the second century in Valentinian Gnosticism for the totality of aeons emanating from God.[30] But according to Valentinian teaching the pleroma is the heavenly fullness to which God does not belong. Hence this understanding of the word cannot contribute anything to the explanation of Col. 1.19, where God himself is called the pleroma. It is a mistake to try to read back such ideas into the New Testament. But it is prossible that one trajectory of development ran from the terminology and theology of Colossians to these later developments in Gnosticism. The more likely background for the phrase *'all his fullness'* is the Old Testament, which recognizes that God himself (or his glory) fills the whole universe (Jer. 23.23), and Wisdom literature, where Wisdom is conceived as pervading all things (Wisd. 7.24). It gives the sense that Christ is thought of as containing, representing, all that God is; and that the destiny of Christians, as the body of Christ, is to enter into that wealth of completeness in him.

1.20 The consequence of this indwelling of God's fullness is described as the reconciliation of the universe: *and through him to reconcile all things to himself*. Although there is no previous mention of it, the presupposition is that the unity and harmony of the cosmos have suffered dislocation, and require reconciliation. However, since reconciliation properly relates only to persons, how can it be applied to the universe?[31] In II Cor. 5.19 Paul seems to be implying that reconciliation has a wider application than believers only. Rom. 8.19–23 too suggests that the whole of the subhuman creation has been subjected to the frustration of not being able to fulfil the purpose of its existence until the redemption of mankind has been accomplished. The universe is reconciled in that heaven and earth have been brought back to their divinely created and determined order. They reach their fulfilment in the redemption that Christ has brought for all who are incorporated into his death and resurrection. According to the author of Colossians this has been brought about, not in some other-worldly drama, but through something done in history, through the death of Christ on the cross.

Making peace through the shedding of his blood on the cross. Now the universe is again under its head, and cosmic peace has been restored. This peace which God has established through Christ binds the whole universe together again. It is at this point that the author of Colossians has added the interpretative phrase or gloss *through the shedding of his blood on the cross*. The effect of this addition is to transform the meaning of reconciliation. The cosmic theology of the hymn proclaimed a universal harmony because of the Creator's work in Christ. It seems that the author of the epistle wanted to relate this more closely to Christ's death on the cross, thereby insisting that redemption comes, not by knowing the cosmic secrets of the universe, but by the forgiveness of sins. This ties up with the setting which the author has provided for the hymn in 1.13f., with its emphasis on forgiveness, and in the application of the theme of reconciliation to the Colossians in 1.21–23. It also shows that the cosmological statements in the first part of the hymn are to be understood in the light of the soteriological statements of the second verse.

As if to drive home further the universal application of this reconciliation in Christ the hymn ends *all things, whether on earth or in heaven*. No part of the cosmos is outside the compass of the divine reconciling work.

The great reconciliation
1.21–23

The author of Colossians continues to expound his theology of atonement in 1.21–23, as he presents a kind of commentary on the hymn of 1.15–20. He returns to the language of direct speech, and interprets and applies the cosmic work of Christ to the readers. In particular the reconciliation, which in the hymn has a cosmic dimension, is here rooted firmly in the experience of the believer and in the life of the Christian community. The effects of this reconciliation, achieved at such cost, could be threatened by shifting from the hope of the gospel they had heard and received. Finally mention of the preaching of the gospel leads on to a consideration of the apostle's ministry. The ministry of reconciliation is paramount. There can be no greater work than bringing together individuals, groups or societies who are estranged to see that their future lies in settling their differences, giving and receiving forgiveness, and accepting one another. Such a ministry has its roots in God's reconciling us to himself through Christ (cf. II Cor. 5.18f.).

1.21 There is a return to direct speech after the liturgical phrases of the hymn, *you yourselves*, to show that the message of reconciliation which embraces all things also applies to the readers. They are described in their pre-Christian state as those who *were alienated from God, his enemies in heart and mind*. The alienation referred to here has been limited by some commentators[1] to refer only to Gentiles. This is certainly how Eph. 2.12 interprets it, transposing the meaning of reconciliation so that one of its major factors becomes the unity of Jew and Gentile in Christ. But here in Colossians the alienation is that which is caused by sin. Such reconciliation is here presented as an already accomplished fact for believers, whereas the cosmic reconciliation of *all things* in the hymn still awaits completion. In Christ the Colossians already have all the benefits of Christ's death.

1.22 *By Christ's death in his body of flesh* is added to demonstrate that reconciliation is accomplished only at the cost of a true incarnation, and of Christ's physical suffering. The expression *body of flesh* is a Hebraism meaning 'physical body'. There is an exact parallel from the literature of Qumran, where the wicked priest is said to have suffered 'vengence upon his body of flesh' (1QpHab. ix.2). The church is the body of Christ because Christ has died for them. It is not possible to belong to the exalted body of the Lord without being baptized into his death.

The object of reconciliation is described: *so that he may bring you into his own presence, holy and without blame or blemish*. The language here is taken from the cultic sacrificial system, where 'holy' and 'blameless' describe the unblemished animal set apart for God. The verb 'to bring' or 'to present' can also be used for the offering of a sacrifice.

1.23 The section ends with a call to perseverance, as the author warns that the effects of reconciliation, achieved at such cost, could be threatened by shifting from the hope of the gospel they had heard and received. The condition, *yet you must persevere in faith* prevents Christian salvation being seen as an experience which is guaranteed for all time. Instead they are to be *firm on your foundations and never to be dislodged*; metaphors of security and strength taken from the picture of a house (cf. Matt. 7.24–27). *Proclaimed in the whole creation under heaven* does not mean that every individual has had the opportunity of hearing the gospel, but that it has been preached in all the great centres of the Roman Empire (cf. Rom. 15.18–20). The fact of the Gentile mission means that the gospel has already been preached world-wide.

There is now a shift to the first person, *of which I Paul became a minister*. The world-wide commission to preach the gospel belongs to Paul. It has been argued that when the title 'minister of the gospel' is here applied to Paul it is the voice of the sub-apostolic age looking back to him as the guarantor of the apostolic office.[2] Although others stand alongside Paul with the title 'minister', such as Epaphras and Tychicus, the scene is set for an idealized picture of the apostolic office of Paul, which could only have come from a later generation.

Minister of the mystery of the gospel

1.24–2.5

The statement that Paul is the minister of the gospel is now expounded more fully in this section. It is in his unique capacity as apostle-minister that Paul, in suffering and in preaching, fulfils the mystery of the gospel. The message entrusted to him is the public proclamation of the now-revealed mystery, of Christ preached among the nations. As apostle he works tirelessly, seeking to teach and warn everyone, with the aim of presenting everyone perfect in Christ. This world-wide activity is encapsulated here in his relationship with the local congregations at Colossae and Laodicea in the Lycus valley.

This idealized view of Paul and of his apostolic office cannot have been written by Paul himself, but comes from the hand of a disciple. It represents a view of ministry and of apostleship that stands halfway between the genuine Pauline letters and the Pastorals. It is almost as if Paul were the only apostle, since Jerusalem and the Twelve are not mentioned.

The passage develops the theme of the gospel and the purpose of the apostle in preaching it. We find two synonymous exprcssions for the gospel, *God's word* (1.25) and *that secret purpose* (1.26f.). Both serve to anchor the work of Christ in God's eternal purpose. There are also some unusual words, 'mystery' (REB *secret purpose*) and 'economy' or 'stewardship' (REB *task assigned*), which are used in a sense different from that found in the genuine Pauline letters, and also different again from their usage in Ephesians.[1] They are tied up with the unfolding purpose of God, as exercised in the preaching of the gospel and the ministry of the apostle.

There are also further links with Wisdom theology. The notion that Wisdom is hidden from this age in the heavenly sphere is found in Jewish apocalyptic literature, including Merkabah texts, where the object of devotion is to induce visions of the throne of God and the angels in their glory. The identification of the mystery of God with Christ in this passage suggests that those who know Christ have no need of further revelation. They have already attained the full riches of complete understanding on the basis of their faith in Christ.

In this passage the relationship of the apostle Paul to Christ and to the church is set out. It is an idealized picture written by an adoring pupil, but is instructive for us in formulating our theology of ministry. Although exclusively concentrated on the work and ministry of the apostle, there is a sense in which he represents the ministry of the whole people of God. This ministry is set out in terms of suffering for the sake of Christ's body, the church (1.24), unfolding the mystery of the gospel as its secret is shared with others in preaching (1.25–29), and building up the church (2.1–5). Preaching and building up the church are of the very essence of ministry. In the course of fulfilling such a ministry there is not a little heartache and suffering. Thus the ministry of the whole church is encapsulated in the work of the apostle.

1.24 This verse is full of problems, expressing ideas for which there seem at first sight to be little parallel in the New Testament, with the possible exception of Ephesians. Both here and in Eph. 1.23 we are dealing with the thought that the church is the complement of Christ.[2] The general idea is that if the church and Christ are one, then the sufferings of the church and Christ are also one; that Christ has not suffered all he is destined to suffer, but goes on suffering in the church; and that Paul is filling up part of the sufferings that are to be completed. This helps to show how, to Paul's mind, Christ in a sense waited for completion, and would find that completion only in the church.

It is now my joy to suffer for you. In the earlier Pauline letters the apostle is not hesitant to mention the sufferings and hardships he has endured for the sake of the gospel.[3] The fact that they are mentioned so frequently might suggest that Paul's sufferings might have been taken as damaging evidence against the truth of his gospel. But here there is an extra dimension, they are *for you*. In what sense were they for the Colossians, a church which Paul had neither evangelized not visited? The real problem is to decide what is meant by *completing what still remains for Christ to suffer in my own person*, a deficiency which is magnified by the obscurity of the language of the verse.

1. At its crudest level the suggestion is that there is something deficient in the redemptive work of Christ to be made up by the suffering of the apostle. This view has been abandoned by all recent

commentators. Notice that the word 'tribulations' is never used of Christ's death on the cross.

2. J.B. Lightfoot[4] is aware of these difficulties, but believes it is still legitimate to speak of Christ's suffering as incomplete, and therefore capable of being supplemented, by making a distinction in the sufferings of Christ between those which represent the passion as the perfect sacrifice for the sins of the world, in which sense there could be no deficiency in the sufferings of Christ, and those which represent those sufferings endured for the building up of the church and for the confirmation of believers in the faith. In this later sense the work of Christ is continued in the sufferings of his people.

3. This could be an allusion to the mystical union with Christ in dying and rising, which binds Christ and the community together so that unity with the Lord allows the whole body of Christ to benefit from the sufferings they experience (Col. 3.1–4; Phil. 3.10). In this connection it should be remembered that Paul suffers, not as a private individual, but as apostle to the Gentiles.

4. A further view draws on the background of Jewish apocalypticism, where it was expected that the coming of the Messiah would be preceded by a period of suffering for the world, and for the righteous in particular. The expected sufferings were referred to as the 'Messianic woes', but were to be of limited duration, like the labour pains of a woman in childbirth (cf. Mark 13.8). In this sense Paul's sufferings could also be said to be those of the Messiah. They were for the sake of the Colossians because they brought nearer the day of their glory. It is almost as if the author is thinking of a fixed quota of sufferings to be endured, so that the more Paul can attract to himself, the less will remain for others. But Colossians is not a conventional apocalyptic writing. The writer does not imagine a new age succeeding this present age. Instead he supposes that believers are already participating in the new age. The divine strategy is to make this known through the apostle and through the church.[5]

5. Moule[6] suggests that if an adequate interpretation is to be arrived at there are two important aspects of the verse that are to be combined. These are: (a) that Christ's sufferings are necessarily shared by Christians; that their union with him involves their participation in his sufferings; (b) that there is a 'quota' of sufferings which 'the corporate Christ', the church, is destined to undergo before the purposes of God are complete. Could it be that the idea of the inclusion of Christians in the 'corporate Christ', the 'more than individual personality' of their Lord, provides the key to the inter-

pretation of the verse? If we think of Christians as being incorporated into Christ by their baptism into him, then it is but a small step to the idea that the sufferings of the corporate body of Christians, the church, and the sufferings of Christ are one; that Christ goes on suffering in the church; and that Paul shares in those sufferings, which he endures not only for the Colossians, but for the whole body.[7]

'In my flesh' may well mean little more than *in my own person*.

1.25 The reference to Paul's suffering leads the writer on to a wider consideration of his apostolic ministry, *I became a servant of the church*. Earlier, in I Cor. 4.1, Paul refers to himself as one of the 'servants of Christ and stewards of the mysteries of God', and in I Cor. 9.17 'I am entrusted with a commission'. Here the word 'commission' or 'office' is used to describe the apostolic commission, *by virtue of the task assigned to me by God* (cf. Gal. 2.9 'the grace that was given to me'). In contrast Ephesians uses the word to mean God's plan of salvation, which is to be completed in the fullness of time (Eph. 1.10; 3.2, 9). The divine office of the apostle is provided for in this plan of salvation. However, the addition of *assigned to me* in Colossians makes it more likely that the reference is to the apostolic commission. The possibility that the word might have the double reference to the apostolic commission and the divine plan, is a further indication that Colossians stands at a point of transition between the undisputed espistles of Paul and the later pseudo-Pauline writings.

The divine commission is to put God's *word into full effect*. The proclamation of the gospel is part of the fulfilling of God's plan, and, like the apostle's taking upon himself an inordinate share of sufferings, is meant to bring nearer the coming of the Lord. The nearest parallel is in Rom. 15.19, where Paul claims that he has completed the preaching of the gospel of Christ' from Jerusalem to Illyricum.

1.26 The apostle's task is to fulfil the word of God and to extend the influence of the saving message. The content of that message is now set out as *that secret purpose hidden for long ages and through many generations*. The term 'mystery' or 'secret' must always be defined by its context.[8] In paganism 'the mystery' was the rite rather than a doctrine. In Judaism it was used of the self-revelation of God in history, the divine secret hitherto concealed, but now revealed by

God. According to the writings of Qumran, such a revelation was granted to the Teacher of Righteousness (1QpHab. vii. 4f.).

In I Cor. 2. 6–10 and 16.25–27, as well as Col. 1.26–27, the mystery does not have to do with some future event that lies hidden in God's plan, but refers to his decisive action in Christ in the present. In fact the content of the mystery (note the singular) is Christ himself. This secret, formerly hidden, is now revealed. In Ephesians (Eph. 1.9; 3.3f., 9; 6.19) the content of the mystery is not so much Christ himself as the inclusion of the Gentiles alongside the Jews in the church.[9] This is a further example of a development of theology between Colossians and Ephesians.

The mystery is not restricted to an inner group of initiates or charismatics, but its contents are made known in the apostolic preaching of the gospel to all nations, to all who will hear and believe. It is *now disclosed to God's people.*

1.27 Several features of the mystery are now outlined. (i) It is splendid in every respect. The accumulation of dependent genitival constructions is typical of Colossians, and here we have another example in the expression a wealth *of glory . . . in this secret purpose.* The words *wealth* and *glory* refer to the greatness of the mystery. In particular 'glory' came to be used in the Septuagint of God's glorious presence, the Shekinah or shining light of his presence.[10] The glory of God is especially present in Jesus Christ. Here in 1.27 *glory* appears twice in quick succession; first of the general splendour of the mystery, and secondly of the final consummation. (ii) The second feature of the mystery is that God has planned to make it known *to the Gentiles* (cf. Eph. 3.2–12). (iii) Thirdly, the actual content of the mystery is *Christ in you,* or 'Christ among you', not in the sense of the indwelling of the Spirit, but the Christ preached among the nations. As the mystery unfolds through the preaching of the gospel it gives *the hope of glory,* an assurance of participation in its final fulfilment.

1.28f. There now follows a short statement about Paul's method as an apostle. Although the writer no longer uses the singular, the plural *we* can mean no one else than the apostle, who is carrying out the commission given to him. *He it is whom we proclaim. We teach everyone and instruct everyone . . .* Three related verbs are used to describe this activity: 'proclamation', which is almost a technical term for missionary preaching, 'admonition' and 'teaching'. The goal of this Christian instruction is *to present each one of you as a mature member of Christ's body*, free from blame or accusation at the last judgment. *Everyone* is repeated three times in v.28 to emphasize the universality of the gospel as taught by Paul and his co-workers.

The apostle exerts himself to declare this message. *I am toiling* does not refer to the manual work which Paul does to earn his own living (Acts 18.3; I Cor. 4.12; I Thess. 2.9; II Thess. 3.8), but the way in which he labours intensely for the welfare of the Christian communities. An even stronger term follows. *Strenuously* is used to describe physical conflict, especially the athletic contest of the Greek games (I Cor. 9.25). Here it is used metaphorically. While Paul strives to fulfil his ministry, he gladly acknowledges that the strength for such labour comes from above, *with all the energy and power of God at work in me*.

2.1–3 The apostle's commission has been outlined in general in the previous verses, but is now applied directly to the Colossians, to the other Christian communities in the Lycus Valley, and *for all who have never set eyes on me*. For them all he has striven greatly, in toil and labour, in inner conflict, and by agonizing over them in prayer. The purpose of this apostolic ministry is to strengthen the readers' hearts. There are textual problems to complicate v.2 in the phrase *God's secret, which is Christ himself*. Later scribes have attempted to clarify the sense by a series of additions and alterations, but the above rendering is the one that can account for all the rest.[11] Here, as in 1.27, the mystery is Christ, but the emphasis has changed. There it was 'Christ in you', here it is 'Christ'. There can be no appreciation of the divine wisdom apart from this personal knowledge of him. All the powers formerly attributed to the personified wisdom of God are now attributed to Christ, *in whom lie hidden all the treasures of wisdom and knowledge*. These treasures are 'hidden', not in the sense that they are kept concealed, but that they exist in Christ, and are unfolded as the gospel is proclaimed.

2.4f. Now for the first time the author expressly points to the danger facing the church, that *no one talks you into error by specious arguments*. The warning is sounded so that the community does not become carried away by the high-sounding words of the deceivers (cf. James 1.22). The danger at hand is not to be underestimated. If he were present at Colossae, the apostle would deal with the situation in person. *I may be absent in body, but in spirit I am with you*, (cf. I Cor. 5.3–5). Because both the apostle and the Christians of Colossae are in

Christ, Paul is present in spirit with them. The condition of the church is described by two terms which have military associations, *unbroken ranks* and *solid front*. Whatever dangers there may be from sophisticated or esoteric perversions of the gospel, the writer has confidence in the spiritual defences of the church.

The death of Christ as a 'putting off' 2.6–15

These verses take us to the heart of the letter. The author recalls the foundation of the Christian life in the person and work of Christ. The claim of the philosophy is to offer the 'fullness' of Christian experience. In response the author points to Christ as the fullness of God himself. They are also recalled to the significance of their baptism in Christ, through which they participate in the benefits of Christ's death. The rules and regulations of the philosophy, parodied as 'empty deceit', 'human tradition' or 'elementary teaching' (v.8) could indeed lead to the stripping off of the flesh and enable the initiate to receive visions of God and of his angelic attendants. But in fact the only stripping off required is the laying aside of the sinful nature in baptism, through which the Christian is united with Christ in his death and resurrection. In him the completeness to which Christians are called is already an accomplished fact. What they possess in him does not need to be supplemented from any other source.

2.13–15 is an almost self-contained unit; a parenthesis on the saving work of Christ. The discussion of baptism, 'the circumcision not made with hands', and its connection with the death of Christ, leads on to the believer's participation in Christ in terms of dying and rising with him, to the forgiveness of sins, and to the celebration of Christ's triumphant death. We have here one of the most important descriptions of what is achieved by the death of Christ, and one of the most emphatic reiterations of the theme of the incorporation of believers in Christ.

Some commentators have detected a liturgical style in these verses, and have suggested that the author has incorporated a liturgical fragment into Colossians to emphasize his argument, composed either by himself, or introduced as an already existing Christian hymn suitably altered to serve his purpose. This is pressing the evidence too far. Any recital of the person and work of Christ is bound to reflect something of the well-used phrases of Christian worship. The liturgical clue would seem rather to lie in baptism, thought of in terms of a death rather than a washing, and the connection of this with circumcision and 'stripping off', again seen as metaphors for death.

This passage is bursting with metaphors as the author draws on a wide range of comparisons in his attempt to express what God has done for us in Christ through his death on the cross. He draws on metaphors and vocabulary from both Jewish and secular backgrounds: (i) fullness, (ii) circumcision, (iii) burial, (iv) dying and rising, (v) the cancellation of a bond of debt, (vi) stripping off of clothing, (vii) the triumphal procession. Of course no metaphor contains the whole truth about its subject, but by a skilful comparison new insights can be given. Such metaphors are not to be taken literally, but accepted for the light they throw on their subject. The preacher and teacher has the task of attempting to expound how the death of Christ relates to us. The metaphors in this passage can be taken up in this way. But it is also an ongoing task in which new metaphors and comparisons can be taken up from contemporary experience and life to help show how the death of Christ relates to us.

2.6f. With the connective particle *therefore*, a transition is made to a new section in which the author gives a careful exposition of his teaching. That teaching, both christological and soteriological, is grounded firmly in the early Christian tradition about Jesus. Several words in these verses give the impression that the author is recalling the basic Christian instruction the Colossians received when they were baptized into Christ. In particular when he says his readers *accepted* Christ Jesus as their Lord, he is not simply reflecting on their personal commitment to Christ, although that is implied, but he uses this semi-technical word to denote the careful handing on of tradition (cf. I Cor. 11.23f.; 15.1–3).

The expression *Christ Jesus as Lord* is possibly an early Christian confession (cf. Rom. 10.9; I Cor. 12.3; Phil. 2.11). In this confession 'Christ' was no longer understood as a title, but was joined to 'Jesus' to form a double name. With the instruction to *live in union with him* the writer moves from the indicative to the imperative.

Then we have a series of four participles to indicate what is meant by 'walking in him'. The metaphors are mixed. Having spoken of a path on which one is to walk, the author moves to the language of horticulture (*rooted*), then to an architectural metaphor. *Faith* here is more likely to mean their adherence to the apostolic gospel than personal trust. *As you were taught* further underlines the importance of loyalty to the received tradition.

2.8 Exactly what is meant by *the elemental spirits of the universe* is by no means clear, and has been the subject of endless debate. The text of the REB is misleading here in that there is no mention of 'spirits' in the Greek text. Basically 'elements' seems to mean 'the component parts of a series', and hence 'the letters of the alphabet', 'the elementary ABC', 'elementary teaching', and 'the elements out of which the universe is composed'. In Heb. 5.12 it stands for the elementary teaching or first principles of the word of God, and in II Peter 3.10 it refers to the material elements out of which the universe is composed. Two meanings for 'elements' prevailed together at the end of the classical period, namely 'elementary ideas' and 'the material elements out of which the universe is composed'. There is no example of its use in the sense of 'spiritual powers' before the fourth-century Testament of Solomon.[1]

Paul uses 'elements' in Gal. 4.3 and 4.9 in a context where the Galatian Christians, who were mainly Gentiles, are being encouraged to accept circumcision and the keeping of the law as essential to being a Christian. The term refers to the restrictions of pre-Christian religion. Before Christ the Jews were confined under the law, and the Gentiles were slaves to the superstitions of paganism. Thus 'the elements' draws attention to something in common to both Judaism and pagan religion, namely their capacity to enslave rather than to liberate. The reference is to elementary teaching bound up with this world and its regulations, and contrary to the freedom of the Spirit. Christians ought to have grown out of such teaching after experiencing their adult status in Christ.

The author of Colossians takes up this reference to 'the elements of the world', with its meaning of 'elementary teaching' of an infantile kind, and uses it with reference to the regulations of the philosophy. It is also used in Colossians in a derogatory sense. In 2.8 the Colossians are warned against those who would seduce them with their teaching. The rare word used actually means 'to carry off as booty', and thus to 'enslave' or 'seduce' by being carried away from the truth. The seductive teaching associated with the 'elementary teaching' is referred to as *hollow and delusive speculations* and *traditions of human teaching*. The philosophy involved is not the critical thinking and discerning knowledge of the classical schools of Greek philosophy, but an esoteric teaching which it is claimed will give the initiate a full insight and knowledge of the heavenly places. In an ironic parody the author says that their philosophy is an empty illusion and without any real content. More than that, it is only a 'human tradition' based on the keeping of regulations, and *not on Christ*.

2.9 The sentence is clearly an explanatory repetition of 1.19, as words from the earlier hymn are taken up and applied to the Colossian congregation. The tense is past there, present here, but in both the reference is to the presence of God in Jesus Christ. The subject of the sentence is also clear – *Godhead in all its fullness*. It is *in Christ* that the divine fullness dwells in its totality. Opinion is divided on the interpretation of *embodied*. It has been taken variously as, (i) 'in bodily form' i.e. incarnate, (ii) 'embodied' i.e. expressing itself through the body of Christ, the church, (iii) 'as an organized body' and not diffused throughout a hierarchy of powers, (iv) 'in solid reality' and not in appearance. The latter is to be preferred: 'in solid reality' or 'actually'.

2.10 *In him you have been brought to fulfilment*. The reception of salvation is here described as 'being filled', a play on words which refers back to the previous verse and to the Christ hymn (1.19) both of which speak of the 'fullness' (of deity) dwelling in Christ. It is possible that the author is employing a slogan from the teaching of the philosophy by which 'fullness of life' was promised to its followers.[2] In contrast he asserts that it is only in Christ that they have been filled, and possess the only fullness that matters.

Of Christ it is said that *Every power and authority in the universe is subject to him as head*. 'Head' is used in the sense of supremacy. 'Power and authority' or 'principalities and powers' are the same as those mentioned in the hymn at 1.16 to denote the angelic attendants around the throne of God. In a context where the Colossians were being encouraged to find 'completion' by visionary ascent to worship with the angels, Christ is set out as supreme over them all, since all the fullness of God dwells in him.

2.11f. Here baptism is introduced as part of the polemic against 'philosophy'. Christ's love for sinful humanity meant that he so identified himself with mankind that he died and rose again as our representative. The vital and effective union with him is expressed in the sacrament of baptism. Dying with Christ is described here in terms of being *buried with him in baptism* (cf. Rom. 6.4). The burial indicates a real, not an apparent, death. Having set out the negative side, the author now turns to the positive. The Colossians have also been raised with Christ through faith in the power of God *who raised him from the dead*.

We can understand why the author should have introduced baptism, with its powerful imagery and links with dying and rising with Christ, but why does he complicate his argument with difficult references to circumcision? It is generally agreed that the proponents of the 'philosophy' were using the language of 'circumcision' to describe part of their religious experience. It is possible that they referred to 'circumcision', not as the sign of admission to the Old Covenant, but of the symbolic stripping off of the flesh and release from the body to experience visions.

The Colossians are reminded that they have no need of submission to Jewish ordinances, least of all to circumcision (whether physical or metaphorical), since in Christ they have already undergone a more radical circumcision than the physical rite. They have been baptized into *Christ's way of circumcision* on the cross. Many commentators interpret 'the circumcision of Christ' as 'the circumcision which belongs to Christ' in contrast to the circumcision which belongs to Moses and the patriarchs, and thus as a periphrasis for baptism.[3] But the fulfilment of circumcision is the Christian's participation in the death and resurrection of Christ. This is reached by way of baptism, but it is the ultimate reality with which the author begins rather than the means. As an alternative it is possible to take 'the circumcision of Christ' as an objective genitive, meaning the body of flesh was stripped off when Christ was circumcised. Although v.12 speaks of baptismal participation in the death of Christ, the preceding statement lays unmistakable emphasis on the suffering of death by Christ himself. Here is a circumcision which entailed the stripping off not of a small portion of flesh, but the whole body – a gruesome figure for death.[4] The two phrases *the stripping away of the old nature* and 'the circumcision of Christ' both refer to his death on the cross. Christ's body was stripped off in his death, he was buried, he was raised, and in him the Colossian Christians also stripped off their body of flesh, were buried with him in baptism, and were raised with him therein. The emphasis in all this lies on Christ's act of self-giving in death and the participation of Christians therein. Undoubtedly the description of Christ's death as a circumcision is figurative, but it is used to demonstrate that no further circumcision is required by the Colossian Christians. The sacramental means by which this victory becomes theirs is baptism, in which the vital ingredient is faith.

2.13 The author's link between circumcision and baptism, both of which are interpreted in terms of belonging to Christ in his death, is taken up here and developed. The implications of Christ's death are applied to the Colossians by way of the metaphor of dying and rising with Christ, the contrast between circumcision and uncircumcision, and the resulting forgiveness of sins. *And although you were dead because of your sins . . . he has brought you to life with Christ*. It has been claimed that the clue to Pauline theology lies in what has been called 'Christ mysticism',[5] expressed in such terms as being 'in Christ' and 'dying and rising with Christ'. As a consequence of being 'in Christ' the participant is freed from sin and the law, possesses the Spirit of Christ, and is assured of the resurrection. But how does this become a reality in the life of believers? It has to do with the Pauline conception of the church as the body of Christ. Believers enter this community of God by baptism, and thereby share in the death and resurrection of Christ by being part of the body of Christ. The emphasis is not on an imitation of Christ, but on a participation with Christ in the effects of his death and resurrection. The image of dying and rising with Christ is one of those motifs which the author takes for granted. Linked with the language of participation and set in a baptismal context, it is concerned with the 'how' of belonging to Christ.

Your uncircumcision. Circumcision refers to the Jewish ceremony, involving a minor surgical operation, which came to be regarded as a sign of incorporation into the life and identity of the people of God, and as a seal of the covenant with Abraham. At the time of the Babylonian exile circumcision came to serve as a badge of identity.

Just as circumcision was a term used generally to denote Jews, so 'uncircumcision' was used to refer to the Gentiles.[6] It means literally 'foreskin', and is used of the state of not being circumcised, and thus of Gentiles as distinct from Jews. In 2.13 the reference is to 'the uncircumcision of your flesh' or 'human nature'. Although the Gentiles were literally uncircumcised, it is not the external fact of their uncircumcision, but its symbolic significance that is in mind here. The uncircumcision of the flesh is actually identified with the trespasses which caused their life to become death, and refers to those who have not yet experienced the *circumcision* of 2.11. *Dead because of your sins* and *your uncircumcision* are synonymous phrases. Thus in their pre-Christian state they had not yet come into relationship with the death of Christ, in which they were to find their forgiveness.

The Gentiles were not only physically uncircumcised, but their uncircumcision was a symbol of their alienation from God and from his covenant of grace. One of the striking features of this passage is the linking of circumcision and baptism. Both function as covenant signs, the former as a sign of initiation into the people of God in the Old Testament, and the latter as a sign of admission into the eschatological people of God in the New Testament. *Circumcision* is used in Colossians with regard to participation in the death of Christ in baptism. It relates to the 'how' of the believer's participation in Christ. It is also to do with a sharing in what has already been done by Christ on the cross. Jesus' death there can be called his *circumcision* because the crucifixion was the real and complete laying aside of the flesh, of which circumcision is the partial symbol.

Note the highly Jewish nature of the background. We are dealing not with something imposed on the Colossians by outside Judaizers, as in Galatians, but by fellow-Gentiles who have developed a taste for all things Jewish. It is probable that they were using the vocabulary of circumcision to refer to release from the flesh to experience visions. The author recalls them to the 'circumcision of Christ' in his death, by which alone there is forgiveness of sins.

For he has forgiven us all our sins. Forgiveness is one of the most compelling figures for what is achieved by the death of Christ. But the vocabulary by which this is expressed in the New Testament is something of a problem. In classical Greek the verb is commonly used with the meaning 'to show favour', 'to give freely'. But apart from the examples from the New Testament, the lexicons give no examples of the verb with the meaning 'to forgive'.[7] It is not used of the restoration of broken relationships. Indeed Paul himself normally uses the language of justification rather than forgiveness. But it is a well-known fact that in Colossians there is a marked absence of forensic categories, and a shift to the concept of forgiveness. Why is this so? There must have been something in the Colossian situation to prompt this change. The language of forgiveness represents a view of the relation of God to humanity which carries the strongest moral overtones, and tends to point to a Colossian situation which involved moral behaviour. It also leads naturally to the great metaphor of the cancellation of the cheirograph in 2.14. Certainly the terminology here casts doubt on the Pauline authorship of the epistle.

The change of personal pronouns in this verse from *you* to *us*[8] shows that the author is eager to identify himself with his readers, and claim his share in the trespasses, in order that he might claim it also in the forgiveness. One of the consequences of this is a proliferation of alternative readings, although the correct reading is never really in doubt.

2.14 This verse is concerned with the forgiveness of sins, expressed in terms of the cancellation of a bond. *He has cancelled the bond which was outstanding against us*. It presents a powerful metaphor for the effects of the death of Christ. So much is clear, but problems arise in trying to explain the origin of the metaphor and the grammatical difficulties of the verse.

According to the lexicons a 'cheirograph' is 'a document', 'a certificate of indebtedness', or 'a bond'.[9] In secular literature the word is frequently found in commercial and legal documents. From a study of cheirographs in the papyri E.C. Best concludes that cheirographs are private documents in subjective form.[10] In turning to Colossians he suggests that these essential characteristics of a cheirograph should be kept in view. The interpretation of Col. 2.14 and the use of 'cheirograph' in the Fathers is almost entirely dependent on their exposition of this verse. The varying conclusions to which they come only serve to illustrate the difficulty of arriving at a satisfactory interpretation.

In the New Testament the word 'cheirograph' is found only here in Col. 2.14. The metaphor of the cancellation of the cheirograph has been interpretated in six different ways.

(1) The law of Moses. Eph. 2.15 offers an interpretative paraphrase of Col. 2.14, in which 'legal ordinances' are referred to the law of Moses. The Antiochene Fathers follow this line to take the cheirograph as a reference to a debt to the demands of the law. Col. 2.14 is thus a dramatic way of expressing the cancelling both of our debt and also of the law itself. But can the cheirograph really be a reference to the Old Testament law? It seems hard to imagine how Paul, or a Paulinist, even in a violent metaphor, could have spoken of the law in such drastic terms as *set it aside, nailing it to the cross*. Besides the word 'law' does not occur at all in Colossians. The essential characteristic of a cheirograph is that it is an autograph, written by one's

own hand to authenticate an agreement. This can hardly be applied to the law.

(2) A pact with Satan. Origen understood the cheirograph to mean a bond resulting from personal sin, and went on to suggest that this bond also resulted from mankind's contract with the devil. E. Lohmeyer[11] suggests that the cheirograph is an IOU given by Adam to the devil in paradise, in which he submitted himself to a life of sin and death in exchange for certain benefits which the devil bestowed upon him. But Colossians never mentions the devil, still less a pact concluded with him. For this reason this interpretation, which found only scant support in the Fathers, has not been taken up by any recent commentator.

(3) An IOU from mankind to God. The currently most popular interpretation is that the cheirograph is an IOU from mankind to God. The image is taken from ancient legal and commercial practice. In 2.14 the cheirograph is a certificate of debt, created by the sin of humankind, and autographed by mankind. Irenaeus[12] holds that the bond resulted from Adam's sin, and is passed from Adam to all mankind. In modern times this view was held by J.B. Lightfoot,[13] according to whom the bond in question is signed by the human conscience, by the Jewish people through their failure to keep the law, and by the Gentiles because of their failure to do what they know to be the will of God. This interpretation is good as far as it goes, but seems to lack a specific application to the Colossian situation.

(4) The heavenly book. It has been claimed that there is a Jewish-Christian exegesis of Col. 2.14 behind Odes of Solomon 23.5–9, Gospel of Truth 19.17, and Rev. 5.1–5, according to which the cheirograph is interpreted in terms of a heavenly book.[14] There is evidence drawn from the Old Testament and Jewish literature to show that the idea of such a book of words, kept by God and recalling the sins of mankind, was a familiar theme.[15] It is also claimed that the actual term 'cheirograph' is used of this book in an anonymous apocalyptic writing of the first century BC. In this text the accusing angel held in his hand a book in which was recorded all the sins of the seer. He asked that they might be wiped out. There was also another book containing his good deeds.[16] However the date of the text is uncertain, probably later than the date of Colossians, and certainly from a stage further down the road to Gnosticism than the situation as we see it in the epistle. On this basis we would question its usefulness in determining the meaning of Col. 2.14.

(5) Penitential column. W. Carr[17] draws attention to the penitential columns found in Asia Minor in the second and third centuries AD. These preserve inscriptions which, he claims, fulfil the requirements of a cheirograph. They contain a personal autograph acknowledging indebtedness, and leading to condemnation if the required terms of penitence are not fulfilled. The columns are set up by those who have offended or failed in their religious duties, and in penitence set themselves apart for a period to perform religious functions. The inscription takes the form of a public confession, and glad acceptance of punishment as a sign of the divine forgiveness. Although the earliest examples of such columns come from around AD 126, it is claimed that such public confessions were part of the religious life of Asia Minor in the first century, and would not be unknown to the Colossians. Could the background for the cheirograph be found in such a local religious practice? Carr explains that the crucifixion is the most serious crime of which mankind is guilty, the penultimate line of the cheirograph, the penitential column on which are listed all the crimes of mankind. But the cross, which was the ultimate line in humanity's listed confession, is paradoxically the way of destruction for that indictment of guilt. The greatest flaw in this proposition is that of dating. We cannot be sure that the Colossians knew of the kind of public confession and penitential columns referred to.

(6) Theophany visions. In the Fathers we find a bewildering variety of interpretations of Col. 2.14 and of the cheirograph. This is reflected in the opinions of modern commentators. Eph. 2.15 presents the earliest interpretation of Col. 2.14, but does not actually use the word 'cheirograph'. Other early interpretations in terms of a secret book giving access to the divine realms are found in Gnostic literature. But the Fathers do not take up this idea, probably because of its suspect links with Gnosticism. Even Eph. 2.15 seems to be making a correction of what could be easily misunderstood in a Gnostic direction. Why is this so? The answer may lie in the fact that a later generation saw fit to correct the abuses that the terminology of 2.14, and the interpretation of the cheirograph in a context of theophany visions, could lead to. Of all the Fathers Irenaeus presents the most plausible interpretation of the verse in terms of a metaphor for the cancellation of sin. He is followed by many modern commentators, who take the cheirograph to be a bond of obligation similar to an IOU. However, such a unique metaphor needs to be rooted more clearly in the Colossian situation, so that it would make immediate sense to the recipients of the letter. The missing link could

be the context of heavenly ascent, acceptable in contemporary Judaism, but suspect to a later generation of both Christians and Jews.

We have the idea of a bond or certificate of indebtedness to which all humankind has subscribed because of sin. The link with the theology of mystical ascent is provided by the accompanying phrase *with its legal demands*. This is not a reference to the Mosaic law, but rather to the ascetic rules, dietary regulations, and ordinances concerned with times, seasons and religious festivals referred to in 2.16–23, and regarded as part of the required preparation for those who would experience the visionary ascent of the mystic to witness the worship of the angels in heaven. By his death on the cross Christ has dispensed with the need for subscription to such ordinances, since access to God and the fullness of Christian experience is now available to all Christians through him. The author is making the point to those who would claim that the height of religious experience is to be sought in release from the flesh and ascent to the angel presence of God, that the only putting off of the flesh now required is the putting off of Christ's body in death. All believers are associated with that death in their baptism when they are incorporated into the body of Christ. Hence the great metaphor of forgiveness, the cancellation of debt represented by the cheirograph, dominates this verse.

In the light of this background for the cheirograph, the remaining grammatical and exegetical difficulties of the verse more easily fall into place. The subject of the sentence is properly God, but the close identity of the activity of Christ and God, which is evident throughout the New Testament, makes it possible for the reader to predicate the activity of removing the cheirograph, (and indeed the whole of the action of 2.15) to Christ. The description of what was accomplished on the cross more naturally implies that Christ is the subject.

The twice repeated stress on the hostile character of the certificate of indebtedness overloads the sentence. The phrase *which was outstanding against us* is added to *the bond* as an interpretive clarification. Then the threefold emphasis on the cancellation or removal of the cheirograph shows that God has utterly removed the signed acknowledgement of our indebtedness. 'Cancelling' and *nailing to the cross* further elaborate the removal of the debt signified by *he has set it aside*. There is no evidence that records of debt were crossed out with a letter X, nor for the alleged custom of piercing a cancelled bond with a nail. In fact only one thing was nailed to the cross, namely the body of Jesus. The figure is suggested simply by the crucifixion. It is a vivid way of saying that because Christ was nailed to the cross, our debt has been completely forgiven, rent with Christ's body, and destroyed by his death. We have a glimpse in this metaphor of how Christ's death was effective for us.

The kind of spirituality practised by certain of the Colossians could so easily lead to a neglect of the reality of forgiveness and of the atoning significance of Christ's death. Those who did not embrace such a spirituality would be made to feel guilty, and that their faith was not complete. This is why the author is so keen to lay emphasis on Christ's death as a 'putting off of the body of flesh', and also as a cancellation of the bond of indebtedness nailed to the cross. All Christians share in this.

2.15 This is another verse bursting with metaphorical associations, in which the author continues his exposition of the significance of the atonement in terms of triumph. There are a number of grammatical, syntactical and exegetical problems involved which have led to several alternative marginal readings in the REB. The problems have been identified by J.B. Lightfoot[18] as:

(a) The meaning of the opening participle.
(b) The subject of the action.
(c) The identity of the principalities and powers.
(d) The nature of the triumph and the public display.
(e) The meaning of the final words, 'in him' or 'on it'.

The best way forward is to start with the controlling metaphor, and then to interpret the other variables in the verse in relation to this. The majority of commentators have chosen to start with the meaning of the opening participle, but it is our view that the main action of the verse is concerned with the nature of the triumph and the public display.

THE METAPHOR OF TRIUMPH

. . . and made a public spectacle of them as captives in his triumphal procession. The image is that of a tumultuous procession through the streets of Rome to celebrate a military victory, and the triumphal entry of a military hero into the city of Rome.[19] But one must ask if the main element of a triumph is the parade of defeated and degraded

enemy through the streets of the city? The unquestioned assumption that the 'principalities and powers' in 2.15 are evil beings makes this conclusion inevitable. An alternative view places the emphasis on a festive or celebratory procession,[20] possibly of Dionysian derivation. If this is the case the key theme of a triumph is not that of winning a victory, but the subsequent acclamation of the victor and the celebration. An important study of the origin and development of the triumph by H.S. Versnel[21] throws useful light on what the author of Colossians is trying to convey by his use of this metaphor. The triumph was the highest accolade of honour that Rome could bestow on one of its citizens. It also testified to the power and greatness of Rome. The description of the *triumphator* and of the triumphal procession is particularly instructive for our purpose.[22] The victorious general entered Rome vested in garments of purple and gold, and wearing on his head the *corona laurea*, the symbol of triumph. The spoils of victory and captive prisoners preceded the *triumphator*. His chariot was followed by those Romans who had been liberated from slavery, along with dancers, chorus and rejoicing crowds.

It is our contention that the author of Colossians is using a metaphor which has its origin in the spectacular procession and celebration of the Roman triumph, and that since the emphasis in the event was on the celebratory procession bringing honour to the city, this must be the main force of the metaphor. It accords with the origin of the triumph in a festal procession for Dionysus in Asia Minor. Incidentally those led in triumph by the *triumphator* were not defeated captives, who were driven before the victor's chariot, but liberated Romans, dancers, chorus, and adulating crowds. They are the attendants of the *triumphator* celebrating the fruits of victory in the triumph. If this is the case, the principalities and powers cannot be evil spirit-powers, either despoiled or led in triumph, but part of the celebratory hosts. This also accords well with II Cor. 2.14, where the apostles are depicted as the joyful participants in their commander's triumphal procession, rather than as captives led in shame.

Once the force of the metaphor is settled some of the other details of the verse fall into place. When we think in terms of a celebratory procession, then all associations of shame disappear from the 'public spectacle'.

THE PRINCIPALITIES AND POWERS

Who or what were *the cosmic powers and authorities*? Again the dominance of the military aspect of the triumph, with its emphasis on the parade of degraded captives, has led almost inevitably to the assumption that they are evil spirit-beings who have been despoiled by God (or Christ), and publicly displayed in their weakness and humiliation. It has been further assumed that these were being commended by the Colossian teachers as worthy of placation, and even worship, along with Christ. When it is recognized that the real significance of the metaphor of triumph lies in a different direction, the identity of the principalities and powers becomes an open question. They are in fact the same angelic host of God mentioned in 1.16 and 2.10, as elsewhere in Jewish literature, to establish God's awesome majesty and power. Christ was instrumental in their creation, they have always been his, and now they adore him after his struggle in the public celebration of his splendour. The principalities and powers are the angels of heaven pictured as Christ's army.[23] Certainly there is no mention of a cosmic battle from which Christ emerged as victorious to save men from the spiritual powers of evil. If, as we propose, the Colossians have been engaging in mystical and ascetical practices with the object of witnessing the worship of angels in heaven, there is no need for a reference to the powers of evil to be read into the 'principalities and powers' of 2.15. The object of the reference could then be to show that the celebrations of the angel host can be experienced, not just by an esoteric minority, but by all believers in Christ.

THE DEATH OF CHRIST

The opening participle, translated in the REB, *there he disarmed*, presents the most difficult problem of interpretation in a verse and context which is full of difficulties. It forms the link with 2.14, where the metaphor of forgiveness predominates, and emphasizes the fact that it was through the death of Christ that such forgiveness is made available to the believer, and which is celebrated in the triumph. The triumph is thus the celebration of the results of Christ's death made publicly available for all.

The lexicons give two meanings for the participle,[24] namely 'to disarm' or 'despoil' (citing Col. 2.15), and 'to take off' or 'to strip' as of clothes (citing Col. 3.9). The fact that there are no other examples has led to the suggestion that this was a word first used by the author of

Colossians, possibly even coined by him, with a special purpose in mind when he wrote Colossians.[25] The matter is further complicated by uncertainty about the subject of the action. Is it God or Christ? If God is the subject it can hardly mean anything but 'stripping' in the sense of 'despoiling' or stripping a person of something he is wearing; but if Christ is the subject, then it may mean 'stripping off from himself' or 'divesting himself' (reading the Greek participle as a middle voice). The question remains – of what did Christ divest himself? Either of his flesh or of the principalities and powers? The argument of the Greek Fathers, that the object is the powers of evil, 'which had clung like a Nessus robe about his humanity', is taken by J.B. Lightfoot.[26] But Colossians does not even hint at the suggestion that Christ was clothed with the principalities and powers, still less that they are evil. The alternative is to follow the rendering of the Latin Fathers, who assume the participle refers to the putting off of the body in death.[27] The absence of 'the flesh' or 'the body' in the text has been held to militate against this interpretation, but if the 'putting off' is a bold metaphor for the death of Christ, the text for such an interpretation could be found in the reference to 'the stripping away of the old nature, which is Christ's way of circumcision' in Col. 2.11, and to death as a 'putting off' and a 'putting on' in I Cor. 15.53f. and II Cor. 5.3f. There are also parallels with the putting off and on of vices and virtues in Col. 3.9–10, as well as with the initiation ceremonies of the Isis mysteries.[28]

The suggested setting in which the author refers to the celebratory angels who publicly acclaim the saving death of Christ, is that some of the Colossians were talking in terms of 'stripping off the flesh' in mystical visionary experience. They sought release from the body, induced by ascetic practices, to make their visionary ascent and to witness the worship of the angels in heaven. They possibly referred to this 'stripping off' as a 'circumcision', whether or not they actually commended the physical rite. The author takes up the language of 'stripping off' and refers to 'the circumcision of Christ', 'the stripping off of the body of flesh', and Christ's death itself as the only 'stripping off' required; a once-and-for-all stripping by which the believer has access to God. The celebrating of the angels is not just for a few select initiates, but publicly and for all, as they proclaim the victory of his death. All Christians share in the death of Christ, that gruesome 'stripping off', as they put off the old way of life and put on the new. The experience has ethical implications, also seen in terms of a 'stripping off' and a 'putting on'. Although this terminology was undoubtedly conducive to a Gnostic interpretation, as we read it, it was not overtly Gnostic at this stage.

In the light of this the remaining grammatical problems of the verse can be addressed. Although God is technically the subject of the whole section of 2.13–15, it is not unreasonable to assume a change of subject from God to Christ, so that Christ is the subject of v.15. The final 'on it' would then be a reference to the cross. The following translation is offered:

> Having stripped himself (in death), he boldly made an open display of the angelic powers, leading them in triumphal (festal) procession on the cross.

Having participated in this once-for-all 'stripping off' the Colossians need to turn their attention to making its effects a reality in their quality of life.

The Colossian philosophy
2.16–23

Our knowledge of the situation at Colossae, which occasioned the writing of the letter, is derived largely from this passage. But we are hindered by the cryptic nature of this part of the letter from gaining a clear picture. It is filled with allusions to the teaching and catch-words of the 'philosophy'. The sentences are not easily comprehensible, since it is not always clear where the writer has taken over words from the philosophy and used them polemically, or when the phrases are his own formulation. One thing is certain – an important contribution to this philosophy has been made by the Jewish tradition. These Jewish elements, which derive from practices that were popular in the apocalyptic and mystical tradition, find their counterpart in Hellenistic religion, and were easily interpreted in a syncretisistic framework. We have confirmation of the two elements in the philosophy noticed by J.B. Lightfoot,[1] one Judaic and the other Gnostic.

In the attempt to be more specific we suggest that a starting-point for understanding the Colossian philosophy might be the Jewish tradition of mystical ascent. When taken over by those not fully grounded in the Torah, such speculation could lead to the situation that occasioned the writing of Colossians. The clues are there in the references to 'elementary teaching' (2.8, 20), 'the regulations' (2.16f., 21–23), and 'the worship of angels' (2.18).

ELEMENTARY TEACHING

In spite of the fact that the REB gives the rendering, *the elemental spirits of the universe*, there is in fact no example of 'elements' being used of spiritual powers before the fourth century AD.[2] The two meanings current at the end of the classical period are 'elementary ideas' and 'the material elements out of which the universe is composed'. Following Gal. 4.3 and 4.9,[3] we prefer the rendering 'elementary teaching' of an infantile and materialistic kind – teaching bound up with this world and its regulations, and contrary to the freedom of the Spirit. Christians ought to have grown out of such teaching after experiencing their adult status in Christ. The author of Colossians takes up this reference to 'elementary teaching', and uses it of the regulations of the philosophy. In an ironic parody the author says that their philosophy is an empty illusion without any real content. More than that, it is only a 'human tradition' based on the keeping of regulations, and not according to Christ.

REGULATIONS

In 2.16 and 2.21 we are given examples of the actual regulations being commended. They concern food and drink as well as the observance of religious festivals. But the restrictions went far beyond anything required in the Jewish law, and were part of a stringent ascetic programme. The author disparagingly repeats the prohibitions of the philosophers in their own words as he caricatures their negative nature: *Do not handle this, do not taste that, do not touch the other*. The author derides these regulations as *human rules and regulations* (2.22), and belonging to a transitory order. They are being commended as part of a religious package which included a strict ascetic régime, and could lead to the inducement of visions. But in fact, it was more likely to lead to a spiritual arrogance which is parallel to the indulgence of the flesh.

WORSHIP OF ANGELS

It is in 2.18 that we are given the clue to the identity of the philosophy, especially in the phrase 'angel worship'. What is referred to here is not a literal worshipping of angels which led to a devaluation of the person and work of Christ,[4] but something much more subtle, and something which would not have occasioned the kind of violent reaction that the law/gospel controversy drew from Paul in Galatians. If the 'worship of angels' can be read as a subjective genitive, we have the idea of the initiate entering the heavenly realms to witness the angelic worship of God. There are parallels in the entry of the initiate into the innermost sanctuary of the god in the pagan mysteries, especially the Isis mystery at Claros.[5] It is possible to find a background for these ideas in the Jewish tradition of mystical piety and visionary ascent.[6] The aim of such mysticism is the knowledge of the heavenly realms. This is not easily achieved, hence the necessity of rigorous preparation, with its emphasis on asceticism and ethical rectitude. Such techniques were part of the normal preparation for the ascent of the mystic. The concept of participation in the angelic liturgy was a familiar one in apocalyptic literature and in Jewish Merkabah mysticism. It was not limited to a nonconformist fringe, but was an accepted part of rabbinic piety.[7] It has been suggested that Paul himself, trained in the traditional rabbinic methods of his day, also experienced some kind of visionary mysticism (II Cor. 12.1–4). This is why Colossians, written in the tradition of the Pauline school, is not concerned to condemn visionary experience as such. It was a legitimate part of Jewish religious devotion which seems to have been taken into a Christian context by certain of the Colossians. But techniques like these could so easily lead to a separation between the mystic and others. As soon as a list of requirements is developed, we also find the tendency to disqualify those whose rigours do not match up to the ideal. Nothing is to be gained by such boasting but the division of the church, an unhealthy concentration on the minutiae of the regulations, and a neglect of Christ who is himself the fullness of deity. The epistle seems to be correcting the enthusiasm of those who have been blessed with the vision of angels. Their error consists in boasting about it and suggesting that those not so blessed are second-class Christians.

THE IDENTITY OF THE PHILOSOPHY

It would seem that there is a pattern emerging which can help us in our search for the identity of the philosophy. The total religious package being commended to the Colossians is directed to the end of inducing visions, and is probably associated with the Jewish tradition of Merkabah mysticism. It involves following a strict ascetic régime, and the meticulous observance of rules, regulations and festivals. Although in the right circumstances this can lead to mystical ascent and the participation of the worshipper in the angelic liturgy, such an experience can easily be made an end in itself, a cause for spiritual pride, and a disparaging of those members of the congregation whose spiritual life is on a more mundane level and who do not receive visions. In this way commandments from the Old Testament and religious practices from Judaism such as fasting and the keeping of festivals, all of which are good in themselves, are reduced to the level of mere regulations. The system is referred to as 'simplistic' or 'elementary teaching', even though its adherents parade it as true wisdom, since it side-steps the things of real spiritual depth. Their emphasis was on the exalted and glorified Christ, but they needed to be reminded of the cross by which Christ brought in the great salvation, and through which they received all its benefits in terms of acceptance by God and forgiveness. Those who cannot see this because of their blinkered ascetic piety are simplistic indeed.

What went on at Colossae? Certainly the epistle stands at a crossroads in the development of concepts and vocabulary. At this time there was action and interaction between the developing Gnosis, Jewish mysticism and Wisdom theology, and Christianity.[8] The common factor with the Colossian philosophy is the use of concepts from Jewish Merkabah mysticism. The visionary ascent of the philosophy is one example of how these ideas were developed in a Christian setting. There were parallel developments in Judaism and Gnosticism, as well as the possibility of a cross-fertilization of ideas in a syncretistic environment. At this stage what is happening is not so extreme as to require condemnation out of hand, but the author of Colossians can see some of the dangers that it might lead to. He therefore concentrates his criticism on the vaunting of spiritual pride, and the neglect of soteriology and ethics to which the philosophy, with its excess of regulations and preparation for visions of angels, might lead. What was going on at Colossae was not Gnosticism as such, nor was it just a case of syncretism. We have what looks like an early stage in a trajectory which leads from Jewish mysticism, through contact with Christianity in a Hellenistic environment, to the later Gnosticism of the second century. The reply of the author of Colossians is part of the self-definition of Christianity which was beginning to take place in the last quarter of the first century.

Today we do not speculate about the place of angels in the heavenly orders. Nevertheless there are dangers in exercising our freedom to pursue our religious experience wherever it might lead. There is a need to recognize the bounds within which an acceptable diversity can operate. The bounds are set by an adequate view of incarnation and atonement, backed up by a quality of life that reflects these beliefs.

The Colossian 'philosophers', although they held a high view of the person of Christ, had a tendency to neglect the death of Christ. Their speculation about the glory of Christ and his place in the heavenly orders got out of hand because it was not rooted in the reality of his suffering and death on the cross. Moreover the 'philosophers' also had a tendency to despise others in their fellowship whose religious experience was on a more mundane level, and did not extend to the esoteric.

We can recognize this tendency in modern church life. The claim that a second blessing, a speaking in tongues, a particular charismatic experience, or a claim to be directly guided by the Holy Spirit are essential to a fully authentic Christian life, along with a tendency to relegate those not 'blessed' in this way to a second division is common in certain circles.

The author of Colossians indicates that a full view of the person of Christ and the atonement, backed up by a way of life worthy of Christ, are the things of first importance. The emphasis is on the fact that all Christians participate in the saving death of Christ. The other experiences are extras, not essentials.

2.16 *Allow no one, therefore, to take you to task.* No one has the right arrogantly to set himself up as a judge over others because they do not follow certain regulations *about what you eat or drink, or over the observance of a festival, new moon, or sabbath.* Here we are given examples of the actual regulations being commended to the Colossians. They concern abstention from food and drink, as well as the observance of religious festivals. The prohibitions listed seem to be of Jewish origin, although it is noteworthy that the Jewish law contains little about abstinence from drink. Only Jews kept the sabbath, so it is likely that 'festival' and 'new moon' also have their primary reference to the Jewish calendar. However, 2.21 strongly indicates that the restrictions envisaged went far beyond anything required in the Jewish law, and were part of a stringent ascetic programme. There is a close parallel with Gal. 4.10, where Paul criticizes the Galatians because they 'observe days and months, and seasons, and years'. But whereas in Galatians those admonished are Gentile Christians who did not understand the full implications of taking on the Torah as a way of life, in Colossians we have moved on a stage further to deal with those who are using the prescriptions of the Mosaic law as a means to another end. In the ancient world fasting and abstinence were used as a prelude to receiving visions and divine revelation.[9] What we have here is part of a religious package being commended to the Colossians, and directed to the end of inducing visions. There are close associations with the Jewish tradition of Merkabah mysticism. In post-Jamnian times an elaborate system of ascetic practices, fasting, the eating of special foods, and the recitation of hymns and incantations was developed in order to induce visions, especially the vision of God seen by Ezekiel the prophet.[10]

2.17 The argument now turns on the regulations. *These are no more than a shadow of what was to come; the reality is Christ's*. They belong to a transitory order. To illustrate the transitory nature of such rules, reference is made to the contrast between the 'copy' and the 'original' which derives from Plato. The contrast is between the reality of Christ and the regulations which are only a shadow of the truth. Religious observance expressed in subservience to 'regulations' is a misunderstanding of God's purpose. *What was to come* sets the reference in an eschatological setting. Since Christ has arrived the reality has already come, and the shadow loses its meaning. This is a contrast more characteristic of the epistle to the Hebrews than of Paul.

2.18 This is one of the most elusive verses in the epistle, crowded with problems of interpretation and rare words. Yet it is here that we are given the clue to the identity of the philosophy, especially in the phrase *angel-worship* or 'the worship of angels'.[11] The majority of commentators have taken this as an objective genitive, denoting a literal worship of angels, and which led to a devaluation of the person and work of Christ. But surely the author could not have failed to denounce as idolatry any cult which made an open profession of such worship? What we have in Colossians is obviously something much more subtle, and something which would not have occasioned the kind of violent reaction that the law/gospel controversy drew from Paul in Galatians. However, if the 'worship of angels' is taken as a subjective genitive, a setting within the tradition of apocalyptic and visionary mysticism is possible. The reference will then be to the visionary ascent of the mystic into the heavenly realms to witness the angelic worship of God.

If this is the case we can understand why the author does not condemn such visionary experience as such, since it could be claimed that Paul himself had experienced something similar (II Cor. 12.1–4). But he does see the danger of such a spirituality, since it could so easily result in a claim of superiority on the part of those who practise it, and a disparaging of those whose experience is on a different level. *You are not to be disqualified* is a clear warning that the readers should not allow themselves to be cheated out of their prize,[12] or to be condemned by those who claim a superior esoteric spirituality.

Discussion on the verse took a new turn when its background was sought in the vocabulary of the mystery religions. In 1911 W.M. Ramsay[13] published an inscription from the Temple of Apollos at Claros from the second century AD, in which *access* or 'entering' is used as a technical term for the final stages of the initiation into the mysteries, when the initiate entered the inner sanctuary to the presence of the god. This opened the way for interpreting 'worship of angels' as a subjective genitive, with the suggestion that the initiate entered the heavenly realms to witness the angelic worship of God. M. Dibelius[14] develops this line of thought as the key to the Colossian philosophy, which he took to be a form of syncretistic mystery practice. He argued that the members of the Colossian church, without abandoning their Christianity, joined with non-Christian teachers in a cultic life devoted to the powers. However, in stressing the pagan character of the cult, Dibelius dismissed the possibility of Jewish influence at Colossae.

The interpretation commended by Dibelius dominated the passage for half a century, so that discussion of Col. 2.18 reached an impasse. F.O. Francis[15] attempted to reopen this discussion by viewing the text against a background of ascetic and mystic trends of piety. He suggests that those Colossians who experienced this form of mystical piety were attempting to impose their views on the whole congregation as normative for the Christian life. It is suggested that the three key phrases in the verse are taken from the language of this piety.

(a) *Self-mortification* or 'rigours of devotion'. Although used in Col.3.12 of the Christian virtue of humility, the word is used here in a technical sense of those ascetic practices regarded as a necessary preparation in apocalyptic literature for the initiate to ascend to the heavenly realms. With the flesh subdued the visionary hoped to receive divine revelation, and to enter the heavenly realms.

(b) *Access to some visionary world*, literally 'which he has seen on entering'. Francis holds that this has a wider reference than initiation into the mysteries, and is more than likely to be used of a visionary entry into the heavenly realms to participate in the worship of the angels in heaven.

(c) *Angel worship*, taken as a subjective genitive, tells us what the visionary saw upon entering the heavenly realms. Since the highest office of the angels is to worship and adore God, the goal and object of the heavenly ascent was to witness the worship of heaven and to join the angels in their liturgy. The concept of participation in the angelic liturgy was a familiar one in apocalyptic literature,[16] at Qumran where it was believed that the community on earth had liturgical fellowship with the inhabitants of heaven,[17] in Jewish Merkabah mysticism,[18] and in parts of the New Testament.[19] Such experiences were a legitimate part of Jewish religious devotion, but when used as an occasion for spiritual pride they became a matter of division in the Christian community. They are condemned by the author for the reason that those who practice them are *bursting with the futile conceit of worldly minds*. The epistle seems to be correcting the enthusiasm of those who have been blessed with the vision of angels. Their error consists in boasting about it, and disparaging the faith of those whose experience did not include visions. Their conceited emptiness is no better than materialism.

2.19 The self-inflated pride in these private religious experiences result from not maintaining contact with Christ, the head. They *lose their hold upon the head*. Taking up the head-body relationship again, it is suggested that it is from the head that the body is supported and held together by sinews and ligaments. A person can only adhere to the head in so far as he belongs, as a member of Christ's body, to the church.

2.20 The author recalls the readers to the significance of their baptism, in which they died with Christ 'out of the control of'[20] elementary and worldly teaching. They are therefore set free from living in subjection to such rules and regulations (cf. Col. 2.14).

2.21f. *Do not handle this, do not taste that, do not touch the other*. These are the author's caricature of the rules and regulations being commended by the proponents of the philosophy. It looks as if all three are concerned with matters of food and drink, although there is also the possibility that sexual abstinence could be implied by the first verb. But these things cannot affect a Christian's relationship with God. They are concerned with the perishable objects of the material world which are destined to pass away when used (cf. Mark 7.6f.), since *all perish as they are used*, being but *human rules and regulations*. They are derided as merely human inventions.

2.23 The ultimate criticism of the regulations comes in this verse. The general trend of what the author has to say is clear, but the grammar and structure of the sentence is obscure. The high incidence of rare and obscure words does not help in the search for meaning. Catch-words from the philosophy and a polemic directed against them are closely intertwined. Some exegetes try to account for the difficulty by assuming that the text must have been corrupted very early, and attempt to reconstruct the text. But none of their conjectures is based on sound manuscript tradition.[22] It is therefore incumbent upon us to make the best sense of the text as it stands.

Much revolves around the final clause *sensuality* or 'the indulgence of the flesh'. The majority of the early Fathers regarded this as a description of the Colossians' ascetic practices, with the suggestion that those who commended the regulations do not give to the body the respect accorded to it by God. They despise rather than satisfy it. But this makes the author's response too mild. He is surely doing more than timidly remarking that the regulations fail because they do not hold the body in sufficient honour. Thus the sense 'the indulgence of the flesh' is to be preferred.

What we have here is a sarcastic borrowing from the language of the philosophy. *Forced piety, self-mortification,* and *severity to the body* are being commended as part of a religious package, and could lead to the inducement of visions. The *rules and regulations* of the system being commended *have an air of wisdom* in that they appear to offer a life of self-discipline, but in fact were more likely to lead a spiritual arrogance which is no better than sensual indulgence.

The moral implications of dying and rising with Christ: the Christian way of life

3.1–4.6

It is characteristic of the Pauline epistles that they fall into two parts – doctrine and exhortation. But it is wrong to press the division too far, since theology and ethics are inseparable. It is incorporation into Christ that makes faith and practice one. Colossians is no exception to this rule, having its paraenetic section which takes up almost one third of the epistle, but with clear links back to the teaching and doctrine expounded in the earlier part of the letter. We find traditional lists of vices and virtues, together with the household code, padded out with suitable proverbial sayings, to form a block of moral instruction and exhortation. At first sight it may seem rather surprising to find so much paraenetic material, since the Colossians have just been instructed, *Let no one dictate to you* (Col. 2.20). Are they being asked to take on a new law, a Christian Torah? The way of life commended is based on the conviction that, as Christians, they have died with Christ and have been raised to life with him, and is meant to follow from the fact that they are 'in the Lord'.

It is now accepted that much of the paraenetic material in the epistles had been collected and used in the life of the early church before Paul and those of his school made use of it. The pioneer work in this field was done by P. Carrington[1] and E.G. Selwyn.[2] The moral condition of the Gentile converts made it imperative that a form of ethical instruction should be devised to meet their needs. The Pauline epistles, I Peter, and James all contain paraenetic material, often written in a style in striking contrast to the normal style of the epistles in which they are set. There is a large measure of agreement in the subjects dealt with, and even a small but distinctive vocabulary which is peculiar to this type of writing. It is claimed that these similarities are the result, not of literary dependence, but of each writer drawing on and developing this traditional material in his own way. 'This means that already at an early date the Hellenistic church . . . was regularly demanding from its converts a high ethical standard as the logical outcome of that inner change which they underwent at the time of their admission to the church.'[3] In compiling such material use was made of suitable ideas to hand from Stoic teaching, Rabbinic sources, and words of the Lord.[4]

There are three types of traditional catechetical and ethical material used in Col. 3.1–4.6 – lists of vices and virtues, the household code, and proverbial ethical sayings known as *topoi*. A good case can be made out for supposing that all three types of traditional ethical material are pre-Pauline. If this is so, their usefulness for the interpretation of Colossians will be derived from the context in which the author of the epistle uses them.

LISTS OF VICES AND VIRTUES

There are numerous lists of vices and virtues in the New Testament, especially in the Pauline epistles.[5] Some have tried to trace their origin to similar lists in Stoicism,[6] and others to an early Jewish proselyte catechism.[7] Undoubtedly in any missionary situation there would be a tendency to make up lists of vices and virtues which would reflect the social concerns of the time. Stoics, Hellenistic Jews, and the early Christians engaged in this activity to distinguish the faithful from those outside the faith. But the contents of these lists are so fluid that it is not possible to be certain if there was direct borrowing from either Stoicism or Hellenistic Judaism. In setting out characteristics not befitting the people of God, they are nearer to the spirit of the 'two ways' teaching found in the Didache, the Epistle of Barnabas, and in the Manual of Discipline at Qumran.[8] The New Testament lists are compiled from conventional material drawn from a variety of sources. Each author seems to have engaged in this activity with a freedom which suggests that there was no original catalogue from which they quoted. G.E. Cannon[9] suggests that the one feature they have in common is the inclination to make such lists.

In Colossians each list contains a series of five vices or five virtues, and each series seems to be related to a central theme. The vices listed in 3.5 are all associated with sexual sins, and call to mind the holiness code of Leviticus 18. They are the sins which belong to their pagan past, being vices for which the Jews especially reproached the Gentiles. The vices in the second list in 3.8 are centred on the attitudes and practices which are detrimental to personal relationships, and which could easily develop in the life of the Christian community. In anger, foul talk, or lies, the heathen sins which they had left behind in baptism were creeping in again. The virtues in the third list in 3.12 are those which show how Christians should behave in their dealings with others, and especially with fellow believers. Could they be associated with ways in which Christ was remembered in the gospel tradition? Despite the traditional character of the lists in Colossians, it is going too far to suggest that the exhortations do not have any reference to specific problems in the community.[10] References and flash-backs to the theme of the whole letter are used to interpret this traditional exhortatory material. Indeed the freedom with which the author has drawn up the lists, and the fact that there are few similarities between them and other ethical lists in the New Testament, confirms this point. Of the links with the earlier part of the letter there are three to be mentioned.

1. The lists are set in the context of the theology of dying and rising with Christ. Because believers have died with Christ in baptism, the demand is laid upon them to put to death *those parts of you which belong to the earth* through which the vices mentioned find their expression. The practices and attitudes of the old way of life are to be left behind because their dominion has been broken. There is a necessary tension here because, although the believer is dead to the world with Christ, he still lives in the world and is subject to its temptations. Hence the transition back and forth between the indicative and imperative. The death of Christ is the event to which the epistle to the Colossians returns again and again. Thus the exhortations, *put to death* of 3.5, and *now that you have discarded* in 3.9, are reminiscent of the description of Christ's death in 2.14f. So close is the connection between the believer and Christ, that Christ's death and his resurrection become those of the believer. The lists and their setting are part of the recall to the concrete and down-to-earth nature of Christian ethics, grounded in the theology of Christ's death. Could it be that there was a tendency to neglect these things in a context where too much emphasis was placed on angelic worship?

2. Another link with the earlier part of the letter is the use of *humility* in the list of virtues in 3.12. It is a well known fact that in secular Greek the word-group from which it comes is used to denote 'mean-spiritedness' or 'shameful lowliness'.[11] But as so often the early Christian enhanced a word of diminished meaning to the rank of a new virtue.[12] The sense of 'unselfishness' or 'lowliness of heart and mind' springs from the example of Jesus (Matt. 11.29; cf. Phil. 2.3). In Colossians the word is sandwiched between four virtues

which relate to conduct towards others, and which are a result of belonging to the New Covenant as *God's chosen and beloved people.*

Humility does not appear in any other New Testament ethical list, so it would seem reasonable to suppose that it has been placed here by the author to counter the kind of self-abasement involved as a necessary prelude to receiving heavenly visions. F.O. Francis[13] suggests that in 2.18 and 2.23 it has the wider meaning of 'rigours of devotion', and that these ascetic practices were a kind of 'humility technique' used to induce visions of the heavenly mysteries. Although such techniques might foster a reputation for 'wisdom', the author of Colossians makes it clear that they are of no use at all in combating sensuality (Col. 2.23). Obviously such techniques had led to an overlooking of basic ethical questions, and to an inflated pride which was the exact opposite of the virtue of true lowliness. Thus we find that *humility* is used in a technical sense by the advocates of the philosophy, and that the author of Colossians, by using it in the list of virtues, attempts to draw attention to the only humility which has any real value. It describes the reality of the new humanity appearing in Jesus Christ, and is not to be used as a means to another end.

3. Thirdly there is the link with baptism. As we have seen, the ethical lists in the New Testament have close links with Stoic and Jewish-Hellenistic catechetical material, but it is the setting of the lists in Colossians that provides the link with the theology of baptism as expounded in the earlier part of the letter. In particular the metaphor of the 'putting off' and the 'putting on' of clothing has links with baptism and initiation. The Colossians are exhorted to discard the old habits of their pre-Christian life as one would discard a set of worn-out clothes. The metaphor was widespread in the ancient world. It was used in the mystery religions to interpret an aspect of initiation,[14] and in the Hebrew tradition of an inward and spiritual change.[15]

It is generally supposed that the exhortation to 'put off' and *put on,* together with the terms *old nature* and *new nature,* fit well into the dramatized theology of adult baptism. The literal stripping off of clothes before entry into the water, and the putting on of new white robes after baptism, is traced by G.R. Beasley-Murray[16] to an early date. But, he insists, 'The important feature is that the baptized stripped off an old life and put on a new one.' The baptismal associations of the epistle are beyond doubt, but it is too simplistic and romantic a view to associate the 'putting off' and 'putting on' of Col. 3.9–12 with the divesting and revesting before and after entry into the water at baptism. The vocabulary of 'putting off' and 'putting on' has links with the putting off of the body in death (II Cor. 5.4; Col. 2.15), and the putting on of the resurrection body (I Cor. 15.53f.; II Cor. 5.2–4). Christ puts off his body of flesh in death (Col. 2.15), and Christians too are to put off the body of flesh by incorporation into Christ's death in baptism (Col. 2.11). The Christian way of life follows from the change of lordship involved in being baptized into the death of Christ. Thus the emphasis is not on divesting before entering the water, but on association with the saving and transforming death of Christ. Furthermore, the terms *old human nature* and *new nature* in 3.9f., with their corporate associations, are part of the presentation of the gospel in terms of the two 'Adams' or the two creations. The dying and rising, the putting off and putting on, and the baptism into the death of Christ, are part of the incorporation into the new creation in Christ, the second Adam. These benefits are available to all Christians, and not just to a spiritual élite.

Thus in the theology of dying and rising with Christ associated with the ethical lists; in the viewing of baptism as a death rather than as a washing; and in the putting on of the particular grace of humility after the example of Christ, we have links with the earlier part of the letter.

THE HOUSEHOLD CODE

In Col. 3.18–4.1 we find rules for the orderly conduct of the Christian household, sometimes referred to as the '*Haustafel*'.[17] It sets out the reciprocal obligations of wives and husbands, children and fathers, slaves and masters, in what amounts to a self-contained paraenetic unit. Certainly the section could be lifted from the context without making an awkward break. The style, with its terse, easy-to-remember lines, is that of catechesis. Also there are a large number of words whose only appearance in the New Testament is in the code. All this makes it likely that we are dealing with a code which existed before Colossians was written, rather than one formed on the spur of the moment in response to Colossian disorders.

The form of the code as we have it in Colossians is the earliest surviving example of this sort of teaching in its Christian form. There are scattered injunctions in earlier epistles, but they are addressed to specific problems rather than to the relationships of everyday life. Pagan prototypes were already current, but the outstanding Christian innovation was the stress on the fully reciprocal nature of the duties. M. Dibelius[18] made the first detailed study of the New Testament household codes and their possible antecedents. His thesis is that they are Christianized versions of the ethical instructions found in Hellenistic and Stoic philosophy. He was supported in his search for a Stoic origin to the codes by his pupil, K. Weidinger.[19] Their views carried scholarly opinion for a generation, although E. Lohmeyer[20] had doubts and preferred a Jewish background. There are similarities with Stoic rules, but there are also differences, especially the reciprocal nature of the duties, which confirms Lohmeyer's suggestion of a Jewish-Hellenistic background.

In his extensive study of the Colossian household code J.E. Crouch[21] suggests its *Sitz im Leben* could lie in the sense of liberation involved in the belief that Christians were the agents of the Spirit and living in the last days. The code made a relatively late appearance in the development of Christian paraenetic material, so it cannot be regarded as part of a primitive Christian catechism. Crouch thinks there must have been a general situation within the Hellenistic churches which gave rise to the specifically Christian form of the household code. One of the special features of the Colossian code is that it places the major emphasis on the duties of the subordinate members of the family and on the duties of slaves. As Christians they were to play the role which society expects of them.

The situation that developed in the life of the church at Corinth is presented as an example of the one in which the Christian form of the household code might develop. In the fellowship of the church the social distinctions between slaves and masters began to lose its meaning (I Cor. 7.20–23), and women found a new liberation (I Cor. 7.10–16; 11.6–16; 14.33–36). Freedom in the Spirit could lead to a desire for freedom in every respect. Such enthusiastic activity on the part of women and slaves, along with the conservative reaction they provoked, was not merely a localized or specifically Christian phenomenon. Crouch traces it to a tension between the two religious attitudes represented by Hellenism and the Jewish synagogue. He proposes that the form of the code in Colossians originated in the conservative reaction of a Jewish type of morality to the pneumatic excesses of Hellenistic religiosity. Such excesses threatened the stability of the Pauline churches. The exhortations to the subordinate members are primary, so it is probable that the original concern of the code was with the excesses of women and slaves. As instructions to these groups became more formalized they were expanded to include children. At the same time the Jewish practice of emphasizing the reciprocal nature of these social duties was incorporated in the form of instructions to husbands, father and masters.

Works on the sociological background to the New Testament tend to suggest that what we have here in the household code is an expression of the conservative reaction to the freedom of the Spirit in a subsequent generation, and the attempt to impose a more patriarchal order patterned on traditional Graeco-Roman (and Jewish) family life.[22] However, the Corinthian situation shows that the tensions between the freedom of the Spirit and a more conventional pattern of life was present in the first generation of Christians. If it can be reasonably supposed that the household code existed before the writing of Colossians, its main impact for our purpose would lie in its use in the epistle. Is there any evidence in Colossians that the purpose of the code was to maintain order in a situation where spirit-filled enthusiasm and the desire for freedom threatened church order? Col. 2.18 suggests that some of the congregation were over-concerned with visions, angelic worship, and other extraordinary activities all of which led to an inflated pride and a neglect of mundane ethical issues. The household code is used to recall them to the simple duties of family life and correct social behaviour.

There is no parallel to the Colossian code outside the New Testament. It is therefore legitimate to speak of the code in a limited and relative sense as a Christian creation. It reached this final form, and was incorporated into the epistle to the Colossians to earth the enthusiasm of visionary experience in the moral demands of everyday life.

TOPOI

A third form of paraenetic material to be found in Colossians, identified by D.G. Bradley[23] as *topoi*, are those brief and pithy admonitions which deal with a variety of subjects. They surround the ethical lists and the household code, locating them in the context of general church life in worship and society. They are self-contained units of teaching which have only a loose and sometimes arbitrary connection with the context. They are strung together, sometimes by means of a catch-word, and often without any apparent connection with adjacent *topoi*. They deal with a variety of general subjects related to daily life, and give practical advice on matters of thought and action which have general applicability. In Colossians they consist of instructions about peace (3.15), teaching one another

(3.16), thanksgiving (3.17), prayer (4.2–4), and conduct towards the outsider (4.5–8). All of them are related to the general subject of church life, and bear the marks of stereotyped admonitions dealing with common and recurrent themes. They appear to have existed before the epistle was written, and were incorporated because they were useful to the author in insisting on a firm ethical foundation to Christian life. D.G. Bradley[24] traces the background to a similar usage in Hellenistic ethical literature outside the New Testament, and in Jewish literature of the Hellenistic period. In their Christian form the *topoi* developed in the hands of teachers and preachers who built up a set of stock answers to recurring questions. Their importance in Colossians lies in setting the ethical lists and the household code in a context of worship and everyday life.

Thus in Colossians we find that the paraenetic material, consisting of ethical lists, the household code, and the *topoi*, has antecedents in Hellenistic and Jewish religious life. Here the material is used in its distinctively Christian form. For our purpose the setting is almost more important than the content of the paraenetic material. The setting is the theology of dying and rising with Christ. This involves the putting off and putting on, not only of vices and virtues and a way of life, but also of the whole personality, of the old man and the new man in Christ. The Christian way of life presented here is meant to be an effective counter to those who would neglect the reality of Christ's death for the more glamorous interest in 'visionary experience'. A true view of atonement roots the Christian life in the ethics of everyday living. Far from being an appendix to the main argument of the epistle, the paraenetic material of Col. 3.1–4.6 brings us right to the heart of the meaning of atonement and the significance of the person of Christ which have been dealt with in the earlier part of the letter.

Much of the material in this section seems to be remote from modern life and attitudes, being sexist, paternalistic, and at times simply banal. There is no outright condemnation of the evils of slavery, but an acceptance of it as one of the institutions of the day. Instead relationships are to be transformed by the love of Christ, and by the fact that in the worship and fellowship of the church differences of social status and prestige are to be transcended. Christian behaviour and the new way of life is a necessary consequence of being 'in Christ'.

It is easy to condemn abuses from afar, and pass judgment on other people's moral dilemmas, but not so easy to see the right way forward from our own problems. Apartheid and civil war in far-away places are easy targets for moral condemnation, but the solution to the problems of Northern Ireland or the uneven distribution of wealth are harder to solve because we are involved in them. In that case the right way forward might be one of Christian concern, working to change attitudes, and a long-term hope that a renewed awareness of our humanity might bring about a change in the situation. This is not too far from the approach we see in Colossians, where there is an acceptance of the institutions of the day, but with the seeds of change and reform already sown in the life of the Christian community and in relationships between Christians.

Dying and rising

3.1–4

This passage marks the transition from the doctrinal and polemical part of the epistle to the ethical and paraenetic section. Although doctrine and ethics are interwoven, it is made clear that the Christian way of life follows on from belonging to Christ and being incorporated into him. The starting point is the believer's participation in the death and resurrection of Christ, of which baptism is the sign. *The realm above* and *this earthly life* represent two different ways of life, the details of which are spelled out in the rest of the chapter, and allegiance to two different lordships. In a clear statement of 'realized eschatology' the new life of the believer is set out as a consequence of having already died and been raised with Christ. This is unparalleled in the undisputed Pauline epistles. In them, whereas the death of Christ is a *fait accompli*, their resurrection and life with Christ are still future (Rom. 6.6; 8.1; I Cor. 15.52–54). Here the implication is that the life of the believer is already a heavenly life, even though it is still hidden (3.3). Nevertheless, it is to be worked out in the present in practical ethical terms. In a situation where those interested in the heavenly realm and in visionary ascent believed this stage could be reached by ascetic practices, special knowledge or legalistic observance, the author recalls them to the significance of their baptism into Christ's death and all its implications for their way of life.

3.1f. When they recall their baptism and its meaning, the readers should be aware of their participation in Christ's death and resurrection, and begin to work out its implications in practical terms. The baptismal allusions here are not to washing, but to association with Christ in his death and resurrection, and the consequent participation in the new age. In order to give expression to this association the author of Colossians makes use of the phrase *with Christ*, and also uses a number of compound verbs also beginning with the prefix 'with'.[25] Here he asks, *were you not raised to life with Christ?* This goes beyond the usual Pauline statements, typified by Rom. 6.3–10, where participation in Christ's death is already a reality, but sharing in his resurrection still has a future element to it. But in Colossians eschatology has receded into the background, as union with Christ in his resurrection is presented as having already occurred as a past event, resulting in new existence for Christians in the present. As a consequence they are to seek *the realm above*. What is in view here cannot be reduced simply to an ethical way of life. It is the sphere of resurrection existence that calls for a different pattern of behaviour. It could be asked why the author follows the dangerous course of telling the Colossians to concentrate on the things above, when part of their trouble seems to come from an excessive concentration on the heavenly world. A.T. Lincoln [26] suggests that this could be another instance of the apostle outclassing his opponents on their own ground. Rather than disparaging their concern with the heavenly realm, he redirects it to show that Christ has the supreme position over any powers the Colossians might associate with *the realm above*. Their starting-point was an attempt to secure release from the things of this world to experience the heavenly world. The author of Colossians moves in the opposite direction, beginning with the believer's experience of the resurrection life of Christ, and progressing to an engagement with the practicalities of everyday living. The starting-point is *where Christ is, seated at God's right hand*. Christ's exaltation forms an important element in the earliest Christian preaching, and goes back to the messianic interpretation of Ps.110.1.[27] The allusion to the psalm is added to underline further the supremacy of Christ in the heavenly realm, and that he is the true way to God.

A second exhortation is issued, to pursue *the realm above*, this time with the present imperative, *fix your thoughts on* (cf. Phil. 3.19f.), denoting continuing action. Such action is to spring from the innermost self which has been united with Christ in death and resurrection. The exhortation is heightened by contrast with *this earthly life*. The earth is the sphere of sin and of this present evil age, and the antithesis between *the realm above* and *this earthly life* a way of contrasting spiritual and unspiritual ways. They represent two different ways of life, one determined by the lordship of Christ, and the other by the dominion of sin. There is no suggestion here that the world of matter is evil in itself, or that life on earth is to be disparaged. The emphasis is on what determines the action and the will. Baptism into Christ means that under the lordship of Christ one is free to live for him.

3.3 The old life has been put aside for ever through the death they have died together with Christ. The aorist tense in the original Greek *you died* denotes a past act – a dying to the elements (2.20) and to *this earthly life* (3.2). Their new freedom follows directly from incorporation into Christ. Henceforth their life is *hidden with Christ*. This is part of the mystery or secret plan of God which is being unfolded as the preaching of the gospel rolls back the frontier of darkness. It is presently known to those who participate in Christ, but is to be revealed in all its fullness at the end of time.

3.4 In the only futuristic eschatological reference in the epistle, it is maintained that the believer's heavenly life will be manifested in all its glory only when Christ shall appear. This is not a reference to the appearance that has already taken place (as in 1.26), but to the parousia. Nevertheless, the emphasis is still upon existence *with Christ*. So closely is the life of his people bound up with Christ that he can be called *our/your life*. The textual variation, with some manuscripts reading *our life* and others 'your life' probably arose as a transcriber's correction, made to introduce uniformity with the preceding verse. In writing *our life* the writer is eager to include himself in the blessings of the heavenly life.[28] Such a sharing in the *glory* of Christ suggests a sharing in the resurrection body (II Cor. 5.1–4; Phil. 3.21). Participation in glory is participation in Christ.[29]

'Put off . . . put on'

3.5–17

In baptism Christians have accepted that the old way of life has been put to death, and that they have been admitted to the new life of the risen Lord. The discarding of the old way of life, and the living out of the new life is described in a series of clothing metaphors, associated with the imperatives 'put off' and *put on*. Christian conduct is therefore to spring from incorporation into the body of Christ. The first section of the ethical appeal is primarily negative (vv.5–11), and includes two lists of vices, one relating to sexual sins, and the other to sins of anger. The positive appeal follows (vv.12–17) with references and flashbacks to the earlier part of the letter, which are used to interpret this traditional exhortatory material. Unlike the ascetic regulations insisted upon by the advocates of the philosophy, which were designed to free initiates from the bonds of the flesh, what is being advocated here is a way of life which has its origin in union with and participation in Christ, but works itself out in practical ethics.

3.5 The main ethical section begins with the imperative *put to death*. The claims of false asceticism have already been dealt with earlier in the letter (2.20–23). What is being advocated here is not a mortification of the flesh, but an extermination of the old way of life outside Christ, which they followed before baptism (cf. Rom. 6.11).

But what is meant by putting to death *those parts of you which belong to the earth?* The use of 'parts' or 'members' in this way is without parallel in the New Testament. The associated list of five vices which follows suggests that they are more likely to refer to man's 'bodily members' i.e. 'the use of your limbs for sensuality'[30] than to 'the members of Christ's body'.[31]. The specific vices in this catalogue are not particularly associated with problems in the community, but are taken from traditional lists, and represent those vices for which the Jews reproached the pagans. There are four sins of sexual excess, *fornication* (cf. Gal. 5.19), *indecency* (cf. I Cor. 6.9; Eph. 5.3), *lust* (cf. I Thess. 4.5; Rom. 1.26), and *evil desire* (cf. Gal. 5.16). *Ruthless greed* stands out as the last member of the list, and breaks the sequence by turning attention from sexual vices to a sin of greed. In so far as it leads a person away from God and encourages him to trust in possessions, it is tantamount to idolatry.

3.6f. At the conclusion of catalogues of vices, reference is frequently made to the future judgment (cf. I Thess.4.3–6; I Cor. 5.10–11; Rom. 1.18–32). This is also the case here in the reminder that *divine retribution* is coming because of the human evil. Associations of anger and punishment have been considered out of place in the Pauline tradition of a gospel of grace. This has led to 'divine retribution' or 'wrath' being interpreted in an impersonal way as the inevitable result of sin, rather than in a personal way as an emotion of hostility on the part of God himself. The chief exponent of this view is C.H. Dodd,[32] who speaks of 'some process or effect in the realm of objective facts', 'an inevitable process of cause and effect in a moral universe'. The verb 'to be angry' is nowhere used in the Pauline corpus with God as the subject. According to Romans 1, people begin by choosing wrongly (the creature rather than the Creator), and then end by being unable to distinguish between right and wrong. What they at first choose to do, they are finally unable to avoid, because God does not protect them from the consequence of their own actions. This is seen as the wrath of God.[33] Perhaps Dodd has pressed his case too far. Others have questioned whether the word 'wrath' can be thus detached from God and turned into a merely mechanical consequence of the laws of cause and effect.[34] Whatever 'wrath' means here, it seems to belong to God. But it is also right to refuse to associate it with the emotion of anger and the intention to punish.

The verb 'to walk' is a favourite Pauline metaphor, drawn from Old Testament and Jewish tradition, for a way of life (cf. 1.10 and 2.6).

3.8 The writer once more takes up a clothing metaphor. They are to discard their old way of life like a set of worn-out clothes. Here the vices of the old way of life that have to be put away are represented by a second catalogue of undesirable attributes – *rage, bad temper, malice* and the language which accompanies these things, *slander* and *foul talk*. The verb 'to put away' was used literally with reference to clothes in Acts 7.58, in a metaphorical sense in Rom. 13.12 and Eph. 4.22 (of the putting off of the old body and the putting on of the new in I Cor. 15.53f. and II Cor. 3.2–4). These parallels indicate that it is the entire sinful nature, of which the vices listed are a manifestation, that is to be put off.

3.9f. *Do not lie* continues the series of imperatives, and is linked with the vices of *slander* and *foul talk* of the previous verse, Following

Moulton and Daube, it is possible to understand the Greek participles translated *you have discarded* and *have put on* in an imperative sense[35] as the readers are urged to give up the old nature with its habits, and to put on the new (cf. Eph. 4.22–24). The alternative is to treat the two verbs as true participles, which describe the past event in which the readers have already put off the old nature and put on the new. The imperative is to be preferred. It shows that the Colossians have to begin to work out the ethical implications of being baptized into the new covenant in Christ's death.

The image of putting off and putting on a garment was widespread in the ancient world, and was employed in the mystery religions in order to interpret the action of initiation.[36] But in the Pauline tradition the metaphor illustrates the change of lordship that has taken place in baptism. Believers have been transferred into the dominion of Christ's rule, and are called to live their lives in obedience to him. The baptismal link is therefore far more significant than a literal change of clothing before and after the rite. It has rather to do with association with Christ in his death, as the parallel use of the participle in Col. 2.15 indicates. Likewise the terms *the old human nature* and *the new nature* do not simply describe an individual condition, but also convey deeper, corporate associations, and describe an old and a new order of existence. They are part of the presentation of the gospel in terms of the two Adams, the two creations. Such a putting off of the entire human nature is without parallel outside the Pauline corpus.[37]

This new humanity which Christ both represents and communicates, and is *in the image of its Creator*, is not referring to man's original creation in the image of God (cf. Gen.1.26), but to the recreation of humankind in the new nature of Christ. This is an ongoing process. It is constantly *being renewed*. Moule[38] points out that the present participle means, not so much that the old Adam is gradually transformed into something better, but rather that the new humanity, already existing in Christ, is progressively actualized in the Christian church, until this process culminates in full recognition, in which one is *brought to know God*. This is not the secret knowledge of the Gnostics, available only to the few initiates, but the capacity to recognise God's will and command, and then to do it.

3.11 The new allegiance to Christ as Lord is one that is to transcend all other divisions between man and woman, whether of race, class, or social distinction. Those who are joined to Christ are also joined to others who have a share in the new humanity (cf. Gal. 3.28; I Cor. 12.13). Even circumcision and uncircumcision have lost their meaning (cf. Gal. 6.15). The violent controversy over the place of law and circumcision, as evidenced by Galatians, is now a thing of the past. All that matters in the Christian community is the 'new creation' in Christ (cf. I Cor. 7.22). A *barbarian* was one who did not speak Greek, and a *Scythian* the lowest form of barbarian – both were pejorative terms used by the Greeks. *Christ is all, and is in all* (cf. I Cor. 15.28; Eph. 1.23) is probably an emphatic way of saying that Christ is all that matters.

3.12 As God's chosen ones who have already put on the new humanity, they must now put on the moral character which is characteristic of him. They are to put on such virtues in their capacity as *God's chosen and beloved people*. All these terms are transferred from the Old Covenant to the New, and point to the church as the true Israel.

The list of five virtues show how a Christian should deal with his fellows, and are the opposite of the five vices in 3.8. The most significant word in the list is *humility*. It has been used twice earlier in the letter (2.18, 23) in a different sense to denote the ascetic practices, such as fasting, which were a prelude to receiving visions of the heavenly mysteries. Here, however, it represents the true Christian virtue of lowliness, after the example of Christ, who was himself 'meek and lowly in heart' (Matt.11.29).

3.13 The two Greek participles translated by *be tolerant* and *forgiving* continue the series of imperatives, and stress once more the importance of correct ethical behaviour for Christians. The reason for such gracious behaviour is that *the Lord forgave you*. Some have seen an allusion here to the Lord's Prayer (cf. Matt. 6.12; Luke 11.14), although a different word is used there. Forgiveness of sins has been conveyed in baptism (2.13), and it is such incorporation into Christ that gives both the community and the individual the freedom and readiness not to perpetuate grudges, but to act in graciousness, after the pattern of the new humanity which they have put on.

3.14 The clothing metaphor reaches it conclusion with the exhortation to put on the crowning grace of *love* as a kind of top-coat over all the others. 'Above all' can convey the idea of 'on top of all the other articles of clothing'. For love surpasses everything else that the new man has to put on and to do (cf. I Cor. 13; Rom. 13.8, 13.10). But what is the meaning of the explanatory clause *to bind everything together*. The RSV takes it as a Hebraism, 'the perfect bond', meaning that loves gives cohesion to the perfect life (as Christ gives cohesion to the universe in 1.17), and binds everything together in perfect harmony. The alternative is to take love as the bond that leads to or produces perfection.[39]

3.15 The need to have a Christian community living together in unison and tolerance is further stressed, as the author passes from love to peace. The distinctive phrase *Christ's peace* seems to mean the peace which Christ brings, which is the result of obedience to him, and which acts as a kind of arbiter or umpire in any dispute. It is to *be arbiter in your decisions*. The word 'to rule' (cf. 2.18) is found only here in the New Testament. It referred originally to the function of the umpire who presided at the games and presented the prizes, but came to be used in a more general sense of 'judge', 'decide', 'control', or 'rule'.[40] It is to such a peace that they were summoned *as members of a single body* – presumably a reference to 'belonging to a single organism',[41] but with allusions to the fact that the way of life characterized by both love and peace is made possible only by incorporation into Christ's body. *Always be thankful* could be a summons to a life of thankfulness, or alternatively a heading for the next topic of catechetical instruction in 3.16f. (cf. I Thess.5.16).[42]

3.16f. Appropriate thanksgiving occurs in the hearing and reflection upon the word, and in the songs sung by the community to glorify God. *The gospel of Christ* means the preaching of the gospel, rather than the words and teaching of Jesus. It is to dwell in them *in all its richness*, a phrase used elsewhere in the epistles in statements which describe God's gracious and rich bestowal of gifts (cf. I Tim. 6.17; II Peter 1.11). As the Spirit of God indwells believers, so the Word of Christ should reside in them in such abundance, producing rich blessing. Teaching and instruction, previously mentioned as activities of Paul and his co-workers (1.28), are now to be taken up by the members of the congregation. They are to make their response in song and praise. *Psalms and hymns and spiritual songs* represent the rich variety of praise in the worship of the early church, although it is not possible to distinguish to what each term refers.[43] It is said of these songs presented to God, that they should be sung *from the* heart. The section is summed up in v.17 with a general admonition *Let ... everything you do be in the name of the Lord Jesus* by giving thanks to God through him.

The Christian household

3.18–4.1

The household code, with its admonitions addressed to wives and husbands, children and fathers, slaves and masters, erupts suddenly into the context of the letter as a self-contained ethical section. This is the earliest Christian form of such instruction, although other examples were soon to follow which were not necessarily dependent on Colossians (Eph. 5.22–6.9; I Tim. 2.8–15; 6.1f.; Tit.2.2–10; I Peter 2.13–3.7; and in the Apostolic Fathers). Pagan and Jewish prototypes were already current.[44] It is obvious that traditional ethical material from a variety of sources has been taken up and adapted for use in the Christian communities.

In each pair, the subordinate party is addressed first and exhorted either to submit or be obedient. Then the superior party is also reminded of their responsibility to those entrusted to them. It has been claimed that the Christian innovation in the code is the stress on the reciprocal nature of the duties. Nevertheless, the note of submission is somewhat out of tune with Paul's claim that in Christ 'there is no such thing as Jew and Greek, slave and freeman, male and female' (Gal. 3.28), as Paul's lofty ideals are reduced to such uninspiring and mundane instructions. The Jewish and pagan basis of the code is vaguely Christianized by the addition of such phrases as 'in the Lord'. It remains 'strikingly poor in original Christian material'.[45] There was no attempt to reform Roman society as such, nor to formulate rules to govern Christian society for all time. Instead we have an example of what the sociologists of religion call 'love-patriarchalism'.[46] Household life was to be transformed 'in the Lord' so that each person was seen as precious to God, and husbands, fathers and masters brought to recognize that they had duties as well as rights. But the basic structure of society was not challenged as such. Christianity was more concerned to commend itself as decent and law-abiding, according to the best standards of the day.

The household code seems to have been incoporated into Colossians because of the link with the case of the runaway slave, Onesimus, dealt with in the letter to Philemon. The code in its Colossian form has a longer section on slavery than elsewhere. Without challenging the institution of slavery itself, the code sets out the obligations of slaves and masters in a Christian context.

J.L. Houlden[47] draws attention to the ill-fitting nature of the code in its context. It seems to disturb the flow of the letter, which moved naturally from doctrinal matters to their ethical implications in 3.5–17. The note of thanksgiving in 3.17, which is taken up again in 4.2, could lead one to suppose that the code was inserted into the letter after it was completed. But Houlden draws back from this drastic conclusion on the ground that, although the code sets out an ethical position which is little different from what the thoughtful Jew or pagan might say, the setting is transformed. The starting-point is incorporation into the new humanity in Christ, so that the relationship of the Christian to Christ transforms all other relationships, and provides the context in which they are to be experienced. Given its context in the theology and ethics of the letter the household code is best seen as traditional ethical material included to help root Christian experience in everyday life.

3.18f. *Wives* should *be subject* to their *husbands* in accordance with the conventions of the accepted social order of the day. The addition of *that is your Christian duty* brings such social conventions within the compass of the Lordship of Christ. The husbands are likewise directed to *love your wives*. The admonition *do not be harsh with them* is part of the practical expression of such love within the Christian household.

3.20f. *Children* are commanded to *obey your parents in everything*. Such behaviour is not only proper according to the conventions of society, but is also a Christian duty. *Fathers* have a special responsibility to their children, and are to be on their guard not to irritate or *exasperate* them, thus causing them to *lose heart* and become sapped of self-respect. Although these instructions may seem banal by the standards of today, they were revolutionary in the ancient world in acknowledging the rights of children.

3.22–4.1 In the longest section of the household code, slaves and masters are addressed. The instructions follow the general pattern of the code, which is a call to obedience and submission, rather than protest. There is an obvious contrast between the freedom granted in Christ, and the servitude of slavery. The sting is partly drawn from the inhuman practice of slavery by an emphasis on the reciprocal responsibilities of both slaves and masters, and in the reminder that what they do is all under the lordship of Christ. For the slaves obedience should be genuine, and not *merely to catch their eye*. This expression, not found before in the Pauline corpus (only in Eph. 6.6), is probably of Christian coinage,[48] with the meaning, 'such service as can be seen', or more probably, 'going through the outward motions without a corresponding keenness of will'. The stress is on motives rather than actions. The menial occupation of the slave is given a new direction of dignity when seen *as if you were doing it for the Lord, and not for men*. Whoever serves obediently and fulfils his task will receive *an inheritance* as his reward. Under Roman law a slave could never inherit anything, but already the Colossians have been promised an eternal inheritance in heaven (1.12). There may be a reference back to the inheritance of the Promised Land by those who at one time werc slaves in Egypt.

3.25 refers to the general principle that whoever does wrong will receive the punishment that fits the crime. Of course this is not necessarily true, but the warning seems to have been introduced into the code to enforce the principle of keeping people in the social station to which they have been assigned. The reference is clearly to slaves and not to masters, who are only addressed in 4.1. There is no *favouritism*, i.e. God is no respecter of persons, to whom master and slave are equal. This is another rare word which seems not to appear before the New Testament, and to have been coined in Christian circles.[49]

4.1 The code ends with a brief address to *masters*. They are not commanded to free their slaves, but directed to fulfil their duties towards them considerately, and not to abuse their position of authority over them. The motive for this just and fair treatment is the same as the slaves motive for obeying his master – they both *have a master in heaven*.

General Christian behaviour

4.2–6

This short paragraph, consisting of a loose series of admonitions and exhortations, ends the paraenetic section of the letter. It is addressed to the entire congregation. The opening note of prayer and thanksgiving picks up the theme of 3.17, interrupted by the insertion of the household code. 4.2–4 contains an exhortation to prayer, thanksgiving and intercession, while 4.5–6 gives directions about their relationship with outsiders. Note also the contrast between the passive role assigned to the congregation, who are to watch and pray, and the active role assigned to the apostle in preaching the gospel and making known the mystery, even when 'in bonds'.

4.2–4 The community is exhorted to constant prayer. In particular they are to be watchful, not in the sense of awaiting the parousia, since the hope of an imminent return of Christ has faded into the background in Colossians, but of a general awareness. Their prayer should be one of thanksgiving and praise. When they pray they should also remember the apostle (with his co-workers – note the plural), and the progress of the gospel. The *secret of Christ* is a reference to the content of the apostolic preaching, and *an opening for the gospel* the opportunity for effective evangelism (cf. I Cor. 16.9; II Cor. 2.12). Again the reference to 'bonds' (REB *in prison*), does not necessarily mean that the author was in prison at the time the epistle was written, but is rather a reference to the servitude to Christ which was a hallmark of the apostolic commission. The author refers to the apostle's 'bonds' as a further way of authenticating his message.

4.5f. In both conduct and speech the members of the community should be aware that those outside have a critical eye, and that they should do nothing to cause unnecessary offence. *Use your opportunities to the full* is a general platitude rather than an eschatological reference, and *never insipid* a plea that their conversation should not be dull or insipid.

Personal greetings and postscript
4.7–18

As in all Pauline letters, the final section of Colossians is taken up with greetings. These are personal messages (7–9), greetings from fellow-workers (10–15), and brief instructions (16–17), and a concluding greeting with a postscript in the apostle's own hand (18). In this respect Colossians conforms to the traditional pattern of letter-writing in the ancient world,[1] except that the conclusion is expanded considerably beyond what is normal to include an unusually long list of greetings. Such secondary greetings, conveyed to the recipients of the letter by the author, are frequently found in secular letters of the period, introduced by the formula 'send greetings to'. In the Pauline corpus the longest list of secondary greetings is to be found in Rom. 16.3–16, where some twenty-six people are named, while the shortest in II Cor. 13.13 simply adds, 'all the saints greet you'. Col. 4.7–18 is second only to Rom. 16 in the unusually large number of people named. There may be some significance in the fact that Paul is supposed not to have visited either Rome or Colossae at the time of writing. A personal autographed greeting is found at the end of five Pauline epistles (I Cor. 16.21; II Thess. 3.17; Col. 4.18; Gal.6.11; Philemon 19).

The sociological study of early Christianity has revealed some interesting facts about the socio-economic status of those whose names appear in the greetings of the Pauline epistles,[2] and in particular the personnel of Col. 4.7–18. Although it is not possible to fully describe the social level of the Pauline Christians, there are a number of clues which indicate that they represent a fair cross-section of urban society. The extreme top and bottom of the Graeco-Roman scale are missing, but the levels in between are well represented. The group most represented in the Pauline letters is the free artisan or small trader. In addition there are household slaves, wealthy Jews, women of independent means, and Gentiles attracted to the synagogue regime. Many of these were upwardly mobile, being people whose drive and abilities had taken them beyond the circumstances of their birth. Some were relatively wealthy, but still of low occupational status. The life of the early Christian communities would provide opportunity for their talents to be used and extended, especially in the sphere of organization and leadership.

The personnel mentioned in Colossians and Philemon include those wealthy enough to own slaves, and those with households large enough to accommodate the fellowship of the church (Philemon 1–2; Col. 4.15), a medical doctor (Col. 4.14), and those whose business allowed them to travel as itinerant evangelists (Col. 1.1, 7; 4.7, 10, 12) as well as the slave Onesimus (Col. 4.9; Philemon 16).

The picture emerges of a missionary with a large number of associates. Indeed Paul is scarcely ever found without companions. There are those who appear to work independently of Paul and have their own sphere of mission, such as Barnabas, Apollos, Prisca and Aquila. The large number of associates who work alongside Paul in his sphere of mission, whose names appear in the greetings of the Pauline letters, are often identified by a series of titles and designations. Among these there is a complete absence of terms of prestige and eminence.[3] No colleague of Paul's is ever called prophet, teacher or pastor, let alone elder or bishop. The most common designations are 'fellow-worker', 'minister', 'brother', and 'apostle'. Probably in response to the Lord's command, they eschew all titles of eminence. With reference to their task, they are workers, servants or special messengers. With reference to one another, they are brothers. Some of Paul's fellow-workers are itinerant missionaries associated with him in co-ordinating the work of the Christian communities in his sphere of mission, while others have their base in a local community. As the church moved into the sub-apostolic age such designations as 'fellow-worker' and 'servant' became displaced by titles of greater eminence, brought about by the need to order church life on a wider scale than the co-ordination of mission we witness in the Pauline period.

In Colossians the ministry of the apostle Paul is the only one singled out for special emphasis (1.24–2.5). His associates are referred to as *dear brother* (4.7, 4.9), *trustworthy helper* (4.7), *fellow-servant* (1.8, 4.7), and 'fellow-worker' (Philemon 1). Timothy, Epaphras, Tychicus, Onesimus and Aristarchus are among the apostle's itinerant colleagues, while Philemon and Archippus would seem to have a local ministry in the community addressed in the letters to Colossians and Philemon. Timothy is associated with Paul in the writing of Colossians (1.1).

Some account needs to be given for the fact that almost all the names in the last section of Colossians are also mentioned in Philemon. Philemon 22f. merely mentions the names, saying that they are 'fellow-workers' of Paul, while Col. 4.10–14 comments on each name, except that of Demas. Obviously the two letters are closely related. One explanation is that both were written at the same time and sent to the same Christian community at Colossae. However, since there are strong reasons to doubt the Pauline authorship of Colossians,[4] the alternative is to suggest that the epistle was written by one of Paul's students who must have known and used Philemon. He found a ready-made list of names and information which he could adapt and expand with news from the circle of the apostle's fellow-workers to help authenticate his own letter, as he attempts to apply the insights of Pauline theology to the situation of his own day. This has led E. Lohse[5] to suggest the existence of a Pauline school tradition, based in Ephesus, where the apostle's teaching was applied and developed to meet the changing situation of church life a generation later. The author of Colossians made use of the messages of greeting in Philemon, with added details to make them more vivid, to ensure that his letter would gain a hearing as a message of Paul, and to recommend to the Christian communities the men named as faithful ministers and helpers of the apostle.

This is more than a list of personnel and associates. We are given an inside view of the workings of life in the close fellowship of the early Christian communities. They were intimate groups where all the members were known to each other by name. Local leadership, in the church for which Colossians was written, depended not on title or eminence, but on a willingness to serve. A leading role would be played by those whose house was used for the meeting of the church.

There are hints of differences of opinion – only a handful of Jewish Christians stand with the apostle. This shows that there never was such a thing as the ideal early Christian community untainted by division or doctrinal differences. Indeed we see a mixed bag of Christians with different talents and abilities, sometimes with conflicting interests. The force which held them together was their loyalty to Christ as Lord.

The Christian fellowship was one in which friendship and support extended to all members. There was an acceptance of one another, and in spite of differences a commitment to work and worship together in the one body. The individual Christian community was not to regard itself as an independent and isolated group, but as belonging to a wider 'communion' linked by the ministry of the apostle and his associates. The writing of letters and visitation by the apostle and his close associates helped to underline this sense of a wider 'belonging'. Thus the picture emerges of a diverse community, not without problems, but with an awareness that loyalty to Christ is more important than any other loyalty or commitment. The realization that there was such diversity in the early church can help us make sense of the diversity, differences of emphasis and doctrinal interpretation, and other problems in contemporary church life. Again the unifying force, for us and them, is loyalty to Christ as Lord.

4.7f. *Tychicus* is the first of Paul's fellow-workers mentioned in the greetings, probably because, along with Onesimus, he is to deliver the letter to the Colossians. According to Acts 10.4 Tychicus was a native of the Province of Asia, and one of the delegates chosen to accompany Paul to Jerusalem with the 'collection' taken up for the needy Jewish brethren there. He also appears in Eph. 6.21; II Tim. 4.12 and Tit. 3.12 as the trusted emissary of Paul.

Tychicus is warmly commended to the Colosians as a *dear brother*, like all the members of the community (1.2), although 'brother' might also be used in a more restricted sense of those colleagues who share in Paul's mission (I Cor. 16.19f., Phil. 4.21f.). E.E. Ellis[6] even goes as far as to suggest that 'the brothers' performed a special role as 'letter bearers' (I Cor. 16.11f.; II Cor. 8.16, 20), and exhorters (I Thess. 3.2; II Thess. 3.15; I Cor. 16.12). Along with Epaphras (1.7), he is also a *trustworthy helper* or 'minister'. The term 'minister' originally denoted one who rendered service of a lowly kind.[7] It is not used here of an ecclesiastical office, but of one who discharges a specific ministry, especially with reference to preaching and teaching,[8] whether as an itinerant or local worker. Finally, also like Epaphras (1.7), he is described as a *fellow servant* in the Lord. The designation 'servant/slave' is an indication that he shared in Paul's ministry of servitude to the Lord (Rom. 1.1), rather than that he was in prison with him at the time of writing.

It is Tychicus's special task to convey personal news of Paul, *to let you know how we are* and *to put fresh heart into you*. The congregation would be eager to learn how things were with Paul. Such personal news would be conveyed by word of mouth, while doctrinal and pastoral matters affecting the whole community would be dealt with in the letter. As the apostle's special delegate, *I am sending him to you*

(Philemon 12), Tychicus would also be able to supplement the contents of the epistle by encouraging and admonishing them (cf. 2.2).

4.9 Tychicus will be accompanied by *Onesimus,* who is also described as a *trustworthy and dear brother* (although not 'minister' or 'fellow-servant'). There is no indication in Colossians that Onesimus is the runaway slave whose case forms the subject of the epistle to Philemon. The name means 'useful', and was commonly given to slaves, but the fact that he is referred to as a native of Colossae, *one of yourselves,* and the special emphasis in the household code of 3.18–4.1 on the reciprocal nature of the master-slave relationship, points to such an identification. The way Onesimus is commended suggests that he is to receive a warm reception into the church community. The fact that he also comes with Tychicus further ensures his acceptance. Together they will convey Paul's personal news.

4.10 *Greetings* are now sent to the Colossians from six of Paul's colleagues, three of whom are of Jewish birth (Aristarchus, Mark and Jesus Justus), and three of Gentile birth (Epaphras, Luke and Demas). If, as we have suggested, Colossians is an epistle written in the Pauline tradition by a disciple of Paul, the names found in Philemon 23 have been taken up by the author, and with additional explanatory comments, incorporated here to authenticate his letter as a message from Paul.

The basic meaning of 'to greet' in secular literature is 'to embrace'.[9] It is the normal term for greetings in the New Testament, where it occurs most frequently as an epistolary formula, sometimes as an imperative, when the writer asks his readers to present his greetings from a distance (cf. Rom. 16.3–16; Col. 4.15), and sometimes, as here in 4.10–14, as an indicative, when fellow-Christians deliver their greetings. Such greetings help to give the readers a concrete picture of the situation in which the epistle is written, and to include the friends and associates of the apostle in the fellowship which he enjoys with them.

Aristarchus is the first mentioned associate to send greetings. He also appears in Philemon 24, and is mentioned in Acts as a natlve of Thessalonica and travelling companion of Paul to Jerusalem, and then to Rome (Acts 19.29; 20.4; 27.2). He is described as *Christ's captive like myself.* It is unlikely that he was actually in prison with Paul, and more probable that the word, which means literally 'prisoner of war', is used metaphorically[10] as a title of honour accorded to a small group of associates (cf. Rom. 16.7, Philemon 23, cf. II Cor. 2.4). *Mark, the cousin of Barnabas* joins Aristarchus in sending greetings. He is readily identifiable with the John Mark of Acts 12.12, the native of Jerusalem, who accompanied Paul and Barnabas on the mission from Antioch to Cyprus and Asia Minor, and whose defection caused the break-up of the missionary partnership (Acts 12.25, 13.13, 15.37–39). Later he appears as a fellow-worker of Paul (Philemon 24, II Tim. 4.11), and then as a companion of Peter (I Peter 5.13). It is interesting that Mark should be identified by his relationship with Barnabas, as if Barnabas was a familiar figure to the churches of Asia Minor. Mark is at this stage slowly gaining back his reputation in the Pauline churches, and needs the commendation of his relationship with Barnabas, and the special plea of Paul. The Colossians have already received instructions that if Mark comes to them, he is to be given a hospitable reception. Such instructions, conveyed either by letter or by word of mouth, no doubt came from Paul himself. There was obviously a great deal more communication between the apostle and his churches than has left direct trace in the surviving letters.

4.11 *Jesus Justus* is the only one in the present list who is not also mentioned in Philemon. These three, Aristarchus, Mark and Jesus Justus, are the only Jews among Paul's faithful workers. *Jewish Christians* (literally 'those of the circumcision') is normally taken to mean Jewish Christians generally. There is allusion here to the bitter divisions in early Christianity caused by Paul's preaching of the law-free gospel to the Gentiles. He has been almost deserted by his fellow Jewish Christians, to the point where they can all be mentioned by name. Their continued support is a great comfort to Paul. An alternative interpretation is presented by E.E. Ellis,[11] who claims that the generally accepted definition of 'those of the circumcision' does not accord with the meaning of the phrase elsewhere (cf. Acts 10.45; 11.2; Rom. 4.12; Tit.1.10), and is better understood within the framework of a twofold Diaspora mission (based on the differences between the Hebrews and Hellenists in Acts 6, where the former followed a strict adherence to Jewish laws and cultus, and the latter a more liberal approach). On this hypothesis the reference in our text would be to those Jewish Christian preachers who took a non-proselytizing attitude to the law, and worked alongside Paul as they evangelized the Jews.

4.12f. *Epaphras* sends special greetings, since as a native of the city of Colossae and its evangelist (1.7), he had been associated with them from the beginning. He is referred to as a *servant of Christ*, a title used elsewhere in the epistles only of Paul himself (cf. Rom. 1.1) and of Timothy (Phil.1.1). It probably indicates exceptional service in the cause of the gospel. In Philemon 23 he is also called 'a captive of Christ Jesus like myself'. Part of his ministry involved agonizing over them in prayer (cf. the Gethsemane agony of Jesus in Luke 22.44). The substance of Epaphras' petition is that the Colossians *may stand fast, as mature Christians* to do the will of God. The participle which comes from the root 'to fill', can mean either 'fulfil' or 'fully convince'.[12] Although a case can be made out for recalling the teaching on fullness which runs throughout the epistle, and giving the sense 'filled with everything that is God's will for them'; it is more likely the prayer is that the readers may be 'fully convinced' of the truth of the gospel.[13]

Epaphras receives a further testimony from the apostle that he *works tirelessly* for the readers. It is fruitless to speculate that he needed this special commendation because something had happened which might have put him in a bad light.[14] Rather his labour sets him alongside Paul in his dedication and concern, not only for the Colossians, but also for the communities at Laodicea and Hierapolis.

4.14 The last two greetings come from *our dear friend Luke, the doctor, and from Demas*. They are both mentioned again in Philemon 24 and II Tim.4.10f., although it is only here that we learn of Luke's profession. There is no reason to suppose that Luke was Paul's medical attendant. His profession is mentioned only because it was an unusual one.

4.15 Greetings are now conveyed from the author, via the Colossians, to the church community in the neighbouring city of Laodicea, and in particular to *Nympha*, in whose house the local church met. There is some uncertainty as to whether this is a reference to a man or a woman. The earliest manuscripts had no accents by which the masculine and feminine forms might be distinguished, so the only ancient evidence lies in the personal pronoun which follows. On balance it appears preferable to understand the reference as being to a woman, and render the phrase, 'Nympha and the church in her house.'[15] The masculine pronoun probably made its appearance in the manuscript tradition when a later scribe, considering the mention of a woman's name here rather unusual, altered the 'her' to 'his'.

'House churches' are frequently referred to in the New Testament (cf. I Cor. 16.19; Rom. 16.5; Philemon 2). Church buildings were rare before the third century, and even when they did exist they were at first ordinary houses given over to church purposes. This means that Christian congregations were for a long time generally no larger than could be accommodated in an ordinary house.[16]

4.16 The author expected the letter to be read out to the assembled church, presumably at worship. When this had been done, there should be an exchange of letters with the church at Laodicea, to which a communication had also been sent. The Laodicean letter should be read aloud to the community at Colossae, and the Colossian letter to the Laodiceans. The instruction in I Thess. 5.27 'that this letter be read to all the brethren', shows that the public reading of the apostle's letters to the assembled congregation was established at an early date. If the exchange of letters was also a common practice, the subsequent collection and publication of the Pauline corpus would be made easier.

The identity of the letter from Laodicea has caused much speculation. The preposition 'from' indicates that the letter is at Laodicea, and it had to be sent from there to Colossae,[17] and does not mean a letter from the Laodiceans to Paul. It has been suggested that the Laodicean letter is either our epistle to the Ephesians (in Marcion's canon Ephesians is given the title 'to the Laodiceans'), or Philemon.[18] However, no extant Pauline composition seems adequately to fit, so we are left with the conclusion that the letter to the Laodiceans did not survive.

4.17 A special word is directed to *Archippus*. According to Philemon 2 he was a member of Philemon's household, possibly his son, and is given the honorary title 'comrade in arms'. He is exhorted to *carry out the duty entrusted to you in the Lord's service*. This is not a reference to an ecclesiastical office, but to a specific task he is to undertake. We have no means of knowing what this task was. Suggestions that it had to do with the collection for the saints, with the rehabilitation of the runaway slave Onesimus,[19] or with making a stand against the Colossian philosophy, are mere speculation.

4.18 Paul regularly dictated his letters, but wrote the last sentence or two in his own hand to confirm their genuineness (cf. I Cor. 16.21; Gal. 6.11; I Thess. 3.17; Philemon 19). It was his autograph rather than signature that provided this confirmation, and provided a counter to any forged letters sent to his congregations (II Thess. 2.1).

Once again the community is called upon to *remember I am in prison* (literally 'remember my bonds'). This is not a matter of invoking their sympathy, but a way of summoning them to respect his authority (cf. Col. 1.23–25). Remembrance in this context does not mean an invitation to pray for the apostle, but an obligation to heed his apostolic authority.[20] The final invocation *grace be with you* concludes the letter.

NOTES

Introduction

1 See the lists in E. Lohse, *Colossians and Philemon*, 1971, 85–7.
2 M. D. Hooker, 'Were There False Teachers in Colossae?' in *Christ and Spirit in the New Testament*, 1973, 313–31. Much of Hooker's argument depends on Pauline authorship of Colossians, and on a comparison with Paul's practice in other letters. But her main argument, that the existence of false teachers peddling a heretical view of the person of Christ can no longer be assumed, still holds good, even if Pauline authorship is denied.
3 F. O. Francis and W. A. Meeks, *Conflict at Colossae*, 1975; also F. O. Francis, 'The Christological Argument of Colossians', in *God's Christ and His People*, 1977, 192–208. A new and more detailed look at the evidence for mystical piety and mystical ascent in Jewish Apocalyptic Literature is presented by T. J. Sappington, *Revelation and Redemption at Colossae* (JSNTS 53), 1991.
4 Francis and Meeks, *Conflict at Colossae*, 215.
5 J. J. Gunther, *St Paul's Opponents and Their Background: A Study of Apocalyptic and Jewish Sectarian Teaching*, 1973, 3–4.
6 J. B. Lightfoot, *Colossians and Philemon*, 1876^{2}, 73–113.
7 R. Yates, 'Colossians and Gnosis', *JSNT* 27, 1986, 49–68.
8 G. Scholem, *Major Trends in Jewish Mysticism*, 1954^{3}; *Jewish Gnosticism, Merkabah Mysticism and Talmudic Tradition*, 1965^{2}.
9 C. Rowland *The Open Heaven: A Study of Apocalyptic Judaism and Early Christianity*, 1982, 393f.
10 Although see E. P. Sanders, 'Literary Dependence in Colossians', *JBL* 85, 1966, 28–45.
11 G. E. Cannon, *The Use of Traditional Materials in Colossians*, 1983, 11–131.
12 C. F. D. Moule, *Colossians and Philemon*, 1957, 4.
13 J. D. G. Dunn, *Christology in the Making*, 1980, 193f.
14 R. Yates, 'Colossians 2.14: Metaphor of Forgiveness', *Biblica* 71, 1990, 248–59.

15 R. Yates, 'Colossians 2.15: Christ Triumphant', *NTS* 37, 1991, 537–91.
16 E. Käsemann, 'A Primitive Christian Baptismal Liturgy' in *Essays on New Testament Themes*, 1964, 149–68.
17 R. Yates, 'A Note on Colossians 1.24', *EQ* 42, 1970, 88–92.
18 G. E. Cannon, *The Use of Traditional Materials in Colossians*.
19 Tacitus, *Annals* 14.27.
20 M. Kiley, *Colossians as Pseudepigraphy*, 1986, 104.
21 On the dilemma facing Paul, and on the institution of slavery in the Roman world see J. M. G. Barclay, 'Paul, Philemon and the Dilemma of Christian Slave-Ownership', *NTS* 37, 1991, 161–86.
22 Pliny the Younger, *Epist*. 9.21, 24.
23 Ignatius, *Eph*. 1.3.
24 J. Knox, *Philemon Among the Letters of Paul*, 1960, 79–93. His further suggestion that Philemon is the letter to the Laodiceans mentioned in Col. 4.16, and that Archippus is actually the owner of the slave Onesimus, rather than Philemon (49–61) is moving into the realms of unsubstantiated speculation.

1.1–2. Preface and Greetings

1 On the conventions of letter-writing in the ancient world see D. E. Aune, *The New Testament in its Literary Environment*, 1988, 158–82.
2 C. F. D. Moule, 'A Note on APOSTOLOS', *Colossians and Philemon*, 155–9; C. K. Barrett, *The Signs of An Apostle*, 1970; J. H. Schütz, *Paul and the Anatomy of Apostolic Authority*, 1975; K. H. Rengstorf, *TDNT* I, 420–43.
3 E. E. Ellis, 'Paul and His Co-Workers', *NTS* 17, 1971, 449, argues, somewhat unconvincingly, that the recipients of the letter were the group of Paul's co-workers responsible for leadership in the community, rather than the whole community.

1.3–8. Thanksgiving

1 P. Schubert, *Form and Function of the Pauline Thanksgiving*, BZNW 20, 1939.
2 P. T. O'Brien, *Introductory Thanksgiving in the Letters of Paul*, 1977, 67.

3 See W. F. Lofthouse, 'Singular and Plural in St Paul's Letters', *ET* 58, 1947, 179–82.
4 J. H. Moulton/N. Turner, *Grammar of New Testament Greek*, III, *Syntax*, 1963, 228.
5 A. M. Hunter, *Paul and His Predecessors*, 1961, 33–5. He quotes from Macarius, an Egyptian monk of the fourth century, *Homilies* 37: 'Hearing the Lord saying, Take care of faith and hope through which is begotten the love of God and of man which gives eternal life.' However, it is more than likely that this saying was created at the inspiration of the Pauline triad.
6 W. L. Knox, *St Paul and the Church of the Gentiles*, 1938, 149 n.5.
7 K. H. Rengstorf, *TDNT* VI, 406.
8 H. W. Beyer, *TDNT* II, 91f.
9 E. E. Ellis, 'Paul and His Co-Workers', *NTS* 17, 438 and 440.
10 J. L. Houlden, *Paul's Letters From Prison*, 1970, 152f; also Moule, *Colossians and Philemon*, 27 n.1.

1.9–14. Intercession

1 As E. Lohse, *Colossians and Philemon*, 33. Cf T. J. Sappington, *Revelation and Redemption at Colossae*, 193–97.
2 For parallels from Qumran see Lohse, op. cit, 25.
3 E. G. Selwyn, *The First Epistle of Peter*, 1947², 281–5.
4 See P. Benoit 'Hagioi en Colossiens 1. 12: Hommes ou Anges?', in *Paul and Paulinism*, ed. Hooker and Wilson, 1982, 83–99; Sappington, *Revelation and Redemption at Colossae*, 199.
5 Käsemann, *Essays on NT Themes*, 154f.; G. E. Cannon, *The Use of Traditional Materials in Colossians*, 12–19, 36–37.
6 F. Büchsel, *TDNT* IV, 349.
7 D. Hill, *Greek Words and Hebrew Meanings: Studies in the Semantics of Soteriological Terms*, 1967, 71–6.
8 D. Hill, *op. cit.*, 65f, 75.

1.15–20. Hymn: the lordship of Christ in creation and redemption

1 E. Norden, *Agnostos Theos* (1913), 1956⁴, 250–54.
2 E. Lohmeyer, *Die Briefe an Die Philipper, Kolosser und an Philemon*, 1964¹³, 41–3.
3 E. Käsemann, *Essays on NT Themes*, 149–68.

4 J. M. Robinson, 'A Formal Analysis of Colossians 1.15–20', *JBL* 76, 1957, 270–87.
5 E. Bammel, 'Versuch zu Col. 1.15–20', *ZNTW* 52, 1961, 88–95.
6 W. McCown, 'The Hymnic Structure of Colossians 1.15–20', *EQ* 51, 1979, 156–62.
7 C. F. D. Moule, *Colossians and Philemon*, 61.
8 P. Benoit, 'L'hymne christologique de Col. 1.15–20' in *Christianity, Judaism and Other Graeco-Roman Cults*, ed. J. Neusner, 1975, I, 226–63.
9 E. Käsemann, *Essays on NT Themes*, 154–7.
10 C. F. Burney, 'Christ as the Arche of Creation', *JTS* 27, 1926, 169–77.
11 W. D. Davies, *Paul and Rabbinic Judaism*, 1955^2, 150–52.
12 R. P. Martin, *Colossians and Philemon*, 1973, 65.
13 J. D. G. Dunn, *Christology in the Making*, 196.
14 F. O. Francis, *Conflict at Colossae*, 183f.
15 J. A. Ziesler, *Pauline Christianity*, 1983, 124.
16 Moule, *Colossians and Philemon*, 169.
17 N. Turner, *Grammatical Insights into the New Testament*, 1965, 122–4.
18 Dunn, *Christology in the Making*, 189; W. Michaelis, *TDNT* VI, 879.
19 Dunn, *Christology in the Making*, 190.
20 Cf. Col.1.17, 20; 3.11; Rom.11.36; I Cor.8.6; 11.12: 12.6; 15.27f.; II Cor.5.18; Eph.1.10f., 23; 4.10; Heb.1.3; 2.8; Rev.4.11.
21 Cf. I Enoch 41.9, 61.10; II Enoch 20–22; Testament of Levi 3.8; Ascension of Isaiah 7.21.
22 G. H. C. Macgregor, 'Principalities and Powers: The Cosmic Background of Paul's Thought', *NTS* 1, 1954, 17–28; G. B. Caird, *Principalities and Powers*, 1956; W. Wink, *Unmasking the Powers: The Invisible Powers That Determine Human Existence*, 1986.
23 O. Cullmann, *The State in the New Testament*, rev. ed. 1963: C. D. Morrison, *The Powers That Be*, 1960.
24 W. Carr, *Angels and Principalities: The Background, Meaning and Development of the Pauline Phrase HAI ARCHAI KAI HAI EXOUSIAI*, 1981. For a critique of Carr see C. E. Arnold, 'The exorcism of Ephesians 6.12 in recent research. A critique of Wesley Carr's view of the role of evil powers in first-century AD belief', *JSNT* 30, 1987, 71–87.
25 R. Yates, 'Satan and the Failure of Nerve', *New Blackfriars* 52, 1971, 223–8.
26 W. Carr, *Angels and Principalities*, 47–85.

27 S. Bedale, 'The Meaning of Kephale in the Pauline Epistles', *JTS* NS 5, 1954, 680–87.
28 Lohse, *Colossians and Philemon*, 53f.
29 C. F. D. Moule, *Colossians and Philemon*, 68.
30 K. Rudolph, *Gnosis*, 1983, 320–22.
31 See the discussion in M. Barth, 'Christ and All Things', in *Paul and Paulinism*, 160–72.

1.21–23. The great reconciliation

1 Lohse, *Colossians and Philemon*, 62.
2 Käsemann, *Essays on New Testament Themes*, 166f.

1.24–2.5. Minister of the mystery of the gospel

1 See C. L. Mitton, *The Epistle to the Ephesians: Its Authorship, Origin and Purpose*, 1951, 82–97.
2 J. A. Robinson, *Ephesians*, 1904^2, 44.
3 Rom.8.35; I Cor.4.9–13; 15.32; 16.9; II Cor.1.8–10; 4.8–12; 6.4–10; 11.23–29; 12.9–10; Gal.6.17. See R. Yates, 'Paul's Affliction in Asia: II Corinthians 1.8', *EQ* 53, 1981, 241–5.
4 Lightfoot, *Colossians and Philemon*, 164.
5 K. Grayston, *Dying, We Live*, 1990, 136f.
6 Moule, *Colossians and Philemon*, 76.
7 R. Yates, 'A Note on Colossians 1.24', *EQ* 42, 1970, 92f.
8 G. Bornkamm, *TDNT* IV, 802–27.
9 Mitton, *Ephesians*, 89.
10 Turner, *Christian Words*, 186; G. Kittel, *TDNT* II, 242–5.
11 For the evidence see B. M. Metzger, *The Text of the New Testament*, 1964, 236–8.

2.6–15. The death of Christ as a 'putting off'

1 G. Delling, *TDNT* VII, 683 n 85.
2 M. Dibelius, *An Die Kolosser, Epheser, an Philemon*, 1953^3, 29.
3 Lightfoot, *Colossians and Philemon*, 183.
4 G. R. Beasley-Murray, *Baptism in the New Testament*, 1972, 152f.

5 A. Schweitzer, *The Mysticism of Paul the Apostle*, ET 1931, Chs. I, VI.
6 K. L. Schmidt, *TDNT* I, 225f.
7 H. G. Liddell and R. Scott, *A Greek-English Lexicon* 1940[9], 1978.
8 See Moule, *Colossians and Philemon*, 27 n.1, and Blass and Debrunner, *Greek Grammar of the NT*, §22–23, 1961.
9 Arndt and Gingrich *Lexicon of the NT*, 886; Liddell and Scott, *op. cit.*, 1985.
10 E. C. Best, *An Historical Study of the Exegesis of Colossians 2.14*, 1956, 7.
11 E. Lohmeyer, *Die Briefe an die Philipper, an die Kolosser und an Philemon*, 1964[13], 116f.
12 Irenaeus, *Contra Haereses*, 5.17.3.
13 Lightfoot, *Colossians and Philemon*, 197.
14 J. Danielou, *The Theology of Jewish Christianity*, 1964, 19–204; O. Blanchette, 'Does the Cheirograph Represent Christ Himself?' *CBQ* 23, 1961, 306–312; A. J. Bandstra, *The Law and the Elements of the World*, 1964, 158–60; H. Weiss, 'The Law in the Epistle to the Colossians', *CBQ* 34, 1972, 292–314.
15 L. Koep, *Das himmlische Buch*, 1952, 55f.
16 G. Steindorff, *Die Apokalypse des Elias, eine unbekannte Apokalypse, und Bruchstucke der Sophianias-Apokalypse*, 1899, 18f. However, no direct reference to the heavenly book, let alone to a cheirograph, can be detected in the text provided by O. S. Wintermute in *The Old Testament Pseudepigrapha* I, ed. J. H. Charlesworth, 1983, 735–53, which he dates between AD 150–275. The late dating and uncertain reference to a heavenly book makes the evidence suspect and questionable in determining the meaning of Col. 2.14.
17 Carr, *Angels and Principalities*, 55.
18 J. B. Lightfoot, *Colossians and Philemon*, 189–92.
19 Blass and Debrunner, *Greek Grammar of the NT*, 5.1, 148.1.
20 G. G. Findlay, 'St Paul's Use of *thriambeuo*', *Expositor*, 1st series 10, 1897, 403–21; R. B. Egan, 'Lexical Evidence on Two Pauline Passages', *NovTest* 19, 1977, 34–62.
21 H. S. Versnel, *Triumphus: An Inquiry into the Origin, Development and Meaning of the Roman Triumph*, 1970.
22 Versnel, *Triumphus*, chs. 2 and 3.
23 W. Carr, *Angels and Principalities*, 60–66.
24 Arndt and Gingrich, *Greek Lexicon*, 83; Liddell and Scott, *Greek Lexicon*, 184.

25 Turner, *Christian Words*, 356–66.
26 J.B. Lightfoot, *Colossians and Philemon*, 189f.
27 J.A.T. Robinson, *The Body*, 1952, 41.
28 M. Dibelius, 'The Isis Initiation in Apuleius and Related Initiatory Rites' in Francis and Meeks, *Conflict at Colossae*, 61–121.

2.16–23. The Colossian philosophy

1 Lightfoot, *Colossians and Philemon*, 73–113.
2 G.Delling, *TDNT* VII, 683 n.85.
3 R. Yates, 'St Paul and the Law in Galatians', *ITQ* 52, 1985, 105–124; see 114–115.
4 Lightfoot, *Colossians and Philemon*, 196.
5 M. Dibelius, 'The Isis Initiation in Apuleius and Related Initiatory Rites', in Francis and Meeks, *Conflict at Colossae*, 61–121.
6 C. Rowland, *The Open Heaven*, 409; 'Apocalyptic Visions and the Exaltation of Christ in the Letter to the Colossians', JSNT 19, 1983, 73–83; R. Yates, 'The Worship of Angels (Col.2.18)', *ET* 97, 1985, 12–15; Sappington, *Revelation and Redemption at Colossae*, 26–137.
7 G. Scholem, *Major Trends in Jewish Mysticism*, 39–41.
8 R. Yates, 'Colossians and Gnosis', *JSNT* 27, 1986, 49–68.
9 J. Behm, *TDNT* IV, 926. Initiation into the Isis mysteries involved ten days of abstinence from flesh and wine: Apuleius, *Metamorphoses* XI, 23, 28 and 30.
10 Rowland, *The Open Heaven*, 228.
11 R. Yates, 'The Worship of Angels (Col.2.18)', *ET* 97, 1985, 12–15.
12 E. Stauffer, *TDNT* I, 637–9.
13 W. M. Ramsay, 'Religious Antiquities of Asia Minor', *ABSA* 18, 1911, 44–46; *The Teaching of Paul in Terms of the Present Day*, 1913, 283–305.
14 Dibelius in *Conflict at Colossae*, 61–121.
15 F. O. Francis, 'Humility and Angelic Worship in Col.2.18', in *Conflict at Colossae*, 163–95; 'The Background of EMBATEUEIN (Col. 2.18) in Legal Papyri and Oracle Inscriptions', in *Conflict at Colossae*, 197–202.
16 II Enoch 20.3f.; Testament of Job 18–50; Apocalypse of Abraham 17; Ascension of Isaiah 7.37.
17 J. Strugnell, 'The Angelic Liturgy at Qumran, 4Q *Serek Sirot Olat Hassabbat*', *VT* suppl. 7, 1960, 318–45.
18 Rowland, *The Open Heaven*, 271–348.

19 I Cor.11.10; Heb.12.22.; Rev.4.5.
20 Blass and Debrunner, *Greek Grammar of the NT*, 211.
21 A. R. C. Leaney, 'Colossians 2.21–3 (the use of *pros*)', *ET* 64, 1952–3, 92.
22 See the literature cited in Lohse, *Colossians and Philemon*, 125 n.88.

3.1–4.6. The moral implications of dying and rising with Christ: the Christian way of life

1 P. Carrington, *The Primitive Christian Catechism*, 1940.
2 E. G. Selwyn, *The First Epistle of Peter*, Appended Essay II, 363–466, where he compares the ethical sections of Romans, Colossians, Ephesians, I Peter and James.
3 G. B. Caird, *The Apostolic Age*, 1955, 113.
4 A. M. Hunter, *Paul and His Predecessors*, 52–7, 128–31.
5 See the lists in G. E. Cannon, *The Use of Traditional Materials in Colossians*, 54–60, and D. E. Aune, *The New Testament in Its Literary Environment*, 194–6.
6 B. S. Easton, 'New Testament Ethical Lists', *JBL* 51, 1932, 1–12; A. Vögtle, *Die Tugend– und Lasterkataloge im Neuen Testament*, 1936.
7 Carrington, *The Primitive Christian Catechism*, 13–21.
8 Didache 1–6; Barnabas 18–20; 1 QS iii. 13–iv.26.
9 Cannon, *The Use of Traditional Materials in Colossians*, 54.
10 Hunter, *Paul and His Predecessors*, 53f.
11 W. Grundmann, *TDNT* VIII, 1–5.
12 N. Turner, *Christian Words*, 216–18.
13 Francis, 'Humility and Angel Worship' in *Conflict at Colossae*, 163–94.
14 Initiation into the Isis-mysteries is described by Apuleius in his *Metamorphoses* XI 23f., where the initiate is divested and then revested in a clean linen garment. See A. J. M. Wedderburn, *Baptism and Resurrection: Studies in Pauline Theology against its Graeco-Roman Background*, 1987, 334f.
15 Isa. 61. 10; Zech. 3. 3f. W. L. Knox, *St Paul and the Church of the Gentiles*, 138, considers that the whole use of metaphors of clothing was so familiar in the conventional language of Judaism that it could be adopted without any thought of its origin.
16 Beasley-Murray, *Baptism in the New Testament*, 148f.
17 From the name given to it by Martin Luther. In the New Testament the form can be found in Col. 3. 18–4. 1; Eph. 5. 21–6.9; I

Peter. 2.17–3.9; with echoes in I Tim. 2.8–15; 6.1–10; Tit. 2.1–10.
18 M. Dibelius, *An Die Kolosser, Epheser, an Philemon*, 48–50.
19 K. Weidinger, *Die Haustafeln: Ein Stück urchristlicher Paranese*, 1928.
20 E. Lohmeyer, *Die Briefe an die Philipper, Kolosser und an Philemon*, 153–5.
21 J. E. Crouch, *The Origin and Intention of the Colossian Haustafel*, 1972, 120–45.
22 J. Stambaugh and B. Balch, *The Social World of the First Christians*, 55; D. Balch, 'Household Codes' in *Graeco-Roman Literature and the New Testament*, ed. D. E. Aune, 1988, 25–50.
23 D. G. Bradley, 'The *Topoi* as a Form in Pauline Paraenesis', *JBL* 72, 1953, 238–46.
24 Bradley, 'The *Topoi*', 241–3.
25 W. Grundmann, *TDNT* VIII, 781–94; A. R. George, *Communion With God*, 1953, 150–55.
26 A. T. Lincoln, *Paradise Now and Not Yet: Studies in the Role of the Heavenly Dimension in Paul's Thought with Special Reference to his Eschatology*, 1981, 126f.
27 D. M. Hay, *Glory at the Right Hand: Psalm 110 in the Early Church*, 1973.
28 On the textual variant see Moule, *Colossians and Philemon*, 27 n.1.
29 G. Kittel and G. von Rad, *TDNT* II, 232–5.
30 As Moule, *Colossians and Philemon*, 115.
31 Blass and Debrunner, *Greek Grammar*, 147.2: N. Turner, *Grammatical Insights*, 104f.
32 C. H. Dodd, *The Epistle to the Romans*, 1932, 49f.
33 J. Ziesler, *Paul's Letter to the Romans*, 1989, 74f.
34 G. Stahlin, *TDNT* V, 419–47; G. H. C. Macgregor, 'The Concept of the Wrath of God in the New Testament', *NTS* 7, 1960–1961, 101–09; C. F. D. Moule, '"The New Life"' in Colossians 3.1–17, *Review and Expositor* 70, 1973, 481–93, see 488.
35 J. H. Moulton, *Grammar of NT Greek* I, 180–83, argues that the use of the participle for the imperative was a genuine Hellenistic development; and D. Daube, 'Participle and Imperative in I Peter', Appended note in Selwyn, *The First Epistle of Peter*, 467–88, suggests links with Jewish and Rabbinic sources.
36 Apuleius, *Metamorphoses* XI, 23f. See J. G. Griffiths, *Apuleius of Madauros: The Isis Book*, 1975, 70–109.
37 P. W. Van der Horst, 'Observations on a Pauline Expression', *NTS* 19, 1973, 181–7, claims that there is a striking analogy to the

metaphorical use of 'man' as the object of the verb 'to take off' in an anecdote preserved by Eusebius (*HE* xiv 18.26) about the philosopher Pyrrho. Pyrrho taught that, reality being beyond the perception of the senses, men ought to rise superior to those senses; yet he lost no time in escaping up a tree when attacked by a dog. When challenged for inconsistency with his own principles, he excused himself by saying that it was difficult 'to take off the man', meaning, apparently, to doff what is human is us. It is possible, however, that the verb in this context means not 'take off', but 'escape from'.

38 Moule, *Colossians and Philemon*, 120.
39 J. H. Moulton, *A Grammar of New Testament Greek*, N. Turner, Vol.III *Syntax*, 212; G. Delling, *TDNT* VIII, 79. For a full discussion of the debate see E. Lohmeyer, *Die Briefe an die Philipper, Kolosser und an Philemon*, 80–82.
40 E. Stauffer, *TDNT* I, 637f.
41 C. F. D. Moule, *The Origin of Christology*, 1977, 76.
42 As R. P. Martin, *Colossians and Philemon*, 114.
43 Moule, *Colossians and Philemon*, 125, comments 'On the face of it, it is not obvious how one instructs and admonishes with psalms etc.' But anyone who is aquainted with the origin of much early Methodist hymnody in doctrinal controversy will appreciate how hymns can be didactic.
44 See G. E. Cannon, *The Use of Traditional Material in Colossians*, 111–18.
45 M. Dibelius, *An die Kolosser, Epheser und Philemon*, 48f.
46 G. Theissen, *The Social Setting of Pauline Christianity*, 1982, 139.
47 J. L. Houlden, *Paul's Letters From Prison*, 209–14.
48 N. Turner, *Christian Words*, 220.
49 E. Lohse, *TDNT* VI, 787.

4.7–18. Personal greetings and postscript

1 See D. E. Aune, *The New Testament in its Literary Environment*, 'Letters in the Ancient World', 158–82, 'Early Christian Letters and Homilies', 183–225; N. A. Dahl, 'Letter', *IDB* Supplement 538–41.
2 W. A. Meeks, *The First Urban Christians: The Social World of the Apostle Paul*, 1983, 51–73.
3 E. E. Ellis, 'Paul and His Co-Workers', *NTS* 17, 1971, 437–52.
4 R. Yates,'A Re-Appraisal of Colossians', *ITQ* 58, 1992, 95–117.

5 E. Lohse, *Colossians and Philemon*, 175–7.
6 E. E. Ellis, 'Paul and His Co-Workers', 449 n.4.
7 H. E. Beyer, *TDNT* II, 87–9.
8 E. E. Ellis, 'Paul and His Co-Workers', 442.
9 H. Windisch, *TDNT* I, for greetings outside the New Testament 496–8, and in the Epistles 500–502.
10 G. Kittel, *TDNT* I, 196f.; Moule, *Colossians and Philemon*, 136f.
11 E. E. Ellis, '"Those of the Circumcision" and the Early Christian Mission', *Studia Evangelica* 4, 1968, 390–99.
12 G. Delling, *TDNT* VI, 309f.
13 As Moule, *Colossians and Philemon*, 138.
14 As G. E. Ladd, 'Paul's friends in Colossians 4.7–16', *Review and Expositor* 70, 1973, 507–14, see 511.
15 On the debate about gender and alternative readings see J. B. Lightfoot, *Colossians and Philemon*, 242; J. H. Moulton, *A Grammar of New Testament Greek*, Vol.I, *Prolegomena, 48; Moule, Colossians and Philemon*, 28 n 1.
16 R. J. Banks, *Paul's Idea of Community: The Early House Churches in Their Historical Setting*, 1980.
17 Blass and Debrunner, *Greek Grammar*, 437.
18 J. Knox, *Philemon Among the Letters of Paul*, 46. For a full discussion of the possibilities see C. P. Anderson, 'Who Wrote "The Epistle From Laodicea"?', *JBL* 85, 1966, 436–40.
19 J. Knox, *Philemon Among the Letters of Paul*, 49–61, holds that Archippus, and not Philemon, was the owner of the slave Onesimus.
20 O. Michel, *TDNT* VI, 682f.

BIBLIOGRAPHY

I Commentaries on Colossians

Abbott T. K. *Epistles to the Ephesians and to the Colossians* (ICC), Edinburgh: T. and T. Clark 1897.

Benoit P. *Les épîtres de saint Paul aux Philippiens, a Philémon, aux Colossiens*, Paris: Editions du Cerf 1949.

Bruce F. F. *The Epistles to the Colossians, to Philemon and to the Ephesians*, Grand Rapids: Eerdmans 1984.

Caird G. B. *Paul's Letters From Prison*, London: Oxford University Press 1976.

Carson H. M. *The Epistles of Paul to the Colossians and Philemon*, London: Tyndale 1960.

Dibelius M. *An Die Kolosser, Epheser, an Philemon*, Tübingen: Mohr, 3rd ed. by H. Greeven 1953.

Firminge W. K. *The Epistles of St Paul the Apostle to the Colossian and to Philemon*, London: SPCK 1921.

Gnilka J. *Der Kolosserbrief*, Freiburg: Herder 1980.

Harris M. J. *Colossians and Philemon*, Grand Rapids: Eerdmans 1991.

Houlden J. L. *Paul's Letters From Prison*, Harmondsworth: Penguin 1970.

Johnston G. *Ephesians, Philippians, Colossians and Philemon*, London: Nelson 1967.

Lightfoot J. B. *Saint Paul's Epistles to the Colossians and to Philemon*, London: Macmillan, 2nd Edn 1876.

Lähnemann A. *Der Kolosserbrief*, Gütersloh: Mohr 1971.

Lindemann A. *Der Kolosserbrief*, Zürich: Theologischer Verlag 1983.

Lohmeyer E. *Die Briefe an Die Philipper, Kolosser und an Philemon*, Göttingen: Vandenhoeck und Ruprecht, 13th ed., ed. W. Schmauch, 1964

Lohse E. *Colossians and Philemon*, Philadelphia: Fortress 1971.

Martin R. P. *Colossians and Philemon* London: Marshall, Morgan and Scott 1973.

Masson C. *L'epître de saint Paul aux Colossiens*, Paris and Neuchâtel 1950.
Moule C. F. D. *The Epistles of Paul the Apostle to the Colossians and to Philemon*, Cambridge University Press, 1957.
Mussner F. *Der Brief an die Kolosser*, Düsseldorf, 1965.
Moulton H. K. *Colossians, Philemon and Ephesians*, London: Epworth 1963.
O'Brien P. T. *Colossians and Philemon*, Waco: Word Books 1982.
Peake A. S. 'The Epistle to the Colossians' in *The Expositor's Greek Testament*, London: Hodder and Stoughton, 1903.
Pokorny P. *An die Kolosser*, Berlin: Evangelische Verlag 1987.
Schlatter A. *Die Briefe an Die Galater, Epheser, Kolosser und Philemon*, Stuttgart: Calwer 1963.
Schweitzer E. *The Letter to the Colossians*, London: SPCK 1982
Synge F. C. *Philippians and Colossians* London: SCM Press 1951.
Radford L. B. *The Epistle to the Colossians and the Epistle to Philemon*, London: Methuen 1931.
Thompson G. H. P. *The Letter of Paul to the Ephesians, to the Colossians and to Philemon*, Cambridge University Press 1907.
Williams A. L. *The Epistles of Paul the Apostle to the Colossians and to Philemon* Cambridge University Press 1907.
Wright N. T. *Colossians and Philemon* Leicester: Intervarsity Press 1986.

II *General Works*

Anderson, C. P. 'Who Wrote "the Epistle from Laodicea"?', *JBL* 85, 1966, 436–40.
Arnold, C. E. 'The exorcism of Ephesians 6.12 in recent research. A critique of Wesley Carr's view of the role of evil powers in first-century AD belief', *JSNT* 30, 1987, 71–87.
Aune, D. E. *The New Testament in Its Literary Environment*, Cambridge: Clarke 1988.
Aune, D. E., ed. *Graeco-Roman Literature and the New Testament*, Atlanta: Scholars Press 1988.
Arndt W. F., and Gingrich, F. W. *A Greek-English Lexicon of the New Testament and Other Early Christian Literature*, Cambridge University Press 1957.
Bammel, E. 'Versuch zu Col. 1.15–20', *ZNTW* 52, 1961, 88–95.

Bandstra, A. J. *The Law and the Elements of the World*, Kampen: Kok 1964.

Banks, R. *Reconciliation and Hope: New Testament Essays on Atonement and Eschatology presented to L. L. Morris*, Exeter: Paternoster Press 1974.

Banks, R. J. *Paul's Idea of Community: The Early House Churches in their Historical Setting*, Grand Rapids: Eerdmans, 1980.

Barclay, J. M. G. 'Paul, Philemon and the Dilemma of Christian Slave-Ownership', *NTS* 37, 1991, 161–86.

Barrett, C. K. *The Signs of an Apostle*, London: Epworth, 1970.

Barth, M. 'Christ and All Things' in M. D. Hooker and S. G. Wilson, eds, *Paul and Paulinism: Essays in honour of C. K. Barrett*, London: SPCK 1982, 160–72.

Beasley–Murray, G. R. *Baptism in the New Testament*, Exeter: Paternoster Press 1972.

Bedale, S. 'The meaning of Kephale in the Pauline Epistles', *JTS* NS 5, 1954, 211–15.

Benoit, P. 'L'hymne christologique de Col. 1.15–20' in *Christianity, Judaism and Other Graeco-Roman Cults*, ed. J. Neusner, Leiden: Brill 1975, Vol. I, 226–63.

— 'Hagioi en Colossiens 1.12: Hommes ou Anges?' in *Paul and Paulinism*, ed. Hooker and Wilson, 83–99.

Best E. C. *A Historical Study of the Exegesis of Colossians 2.14* (Excerpta e dissertatione ad laurem in Facultate Theologia Pontificae Universitatis Gregoriae), Romae 1956.

Blanchette O. 'Does The Cheirograph of Col. 2.14 Represent Christ Himself?', *CBQ* 23, 1961, 306–12.

Blass F. and Debrunner A. *A Greek Grammar of the New Testament and Other Early Christian Literature* 10th ed., trans. R. W. Funk, Cambridge University Press 1961.

Bradley D. G. 'The *Topos* as a Form in Pauline Paraenesis', *JBL* 72, 1953, 238–46.

Burney C. F. 'Christ as the Arche of Creation', *JTS* 27, 1926, 160–77.

Caird G. B. *Principalities and Powers*, Oxford University Press 1956.

— *The Language and Imagery of the Bible*, London: Duckworth, 1980.

— *The Apostolic Age*, London: Duckworth 1955.

Cannon G. E. *The Use of Traditional Materials in Colossians*, Macon: Mercer 1983.

Carr W. *Angels and Principalities: The Background, Meaning and Development of the Pauline Phrase HAI ARCHAI KAI HAI EXOUSIAI*, Cambridge University Press 1981.

Carrington P. *The Primitive Christian Catechism*, Cambridge University Press 1940.
Charlesworth J. H., ed. *The Old Testament Pseudepigrapha*, Vol.I, *Apocalyptic Literature and Testaments*, London: Darton, Longman and Todd 1983.
Crouch, J. E. *The Origin and Intention of the Colossians Haustafel*, Göttingen: Vandenhoeck und Ruprecht 1972.
Cullmann, O. *Christ and Time*, London: SCM Press, rev. ed. 1962.
— *The State in the New Testament*, London: SCM Press, rev. ed. 1963.
Danielou, J. *The Theology of Jewish Christianity*, London: Darton, Longman and Todd 1964.
Daube, D. 'Participle and Imperative in I Peter' in E. G. Selwyn *The First Epistle of Peter*, 1964², 467–88.
Davies, W. D. *Paul and Rabbinic Judaism*, London: SPCK, 2nd ed. 1955.
Dodd, C. H. *The Epistle to the Romans* (Moffatt NT Commentary), London: Hodder and Stoughton 1932.
Dunn, J. D. G. *Christology in the Making* London: SCM Press 1980.
Easton, B. S. 'New Testament Ethical Lists', *JBL* 51, 1932, 1–12.
Egan, B. S. 'Lexical Evidence on Two Pauline Passages', *NovTest* 19, 1977, 34–62.
Ellis, E. E. '"Those of the Circumcision" and the Early Christian Mission' *Studia Evangelica* 4 (TU 102), Berlin 1968, 390–99.
— 'Paul and His Co-Workers', *NTS* 17, 1971, 437–52.
Findlay, G. G. 'St Paul's Use of *thriambeuo*', *Expositor*, 1st series 10, 1897, 403–21.
Francis F. O. and Meeks W. A. *Conflict at Colossae*, Montana: Scholars Press 1975.
Francis F. O. 'The Background of EMBATEUEIN (Col. 2.18) in Legal Papyri and Oracle Inscriptions'in *Conflict at Colossae*, 197–207.
— 'Humility and Angel Worship in Col. 2.18' in *Conflict at Colossae*, 163–95.
— 'The Christological Argument of Colossians' in *God's Christ and His People: Studies in honour of Nils Alstrup Dahl*, ed. J. Jervell and W. A. Meeks, Oslo Universitesforlaget 1977, 198–208.
Fowl, S. E. *The Story of Christ in the Ethics of Paul: An Analysis of the Function of the Hymnic Material in the Pauline Corpus*, Sheffield: JSOT Press 1990.
George, A. R. *Communion With God in the New Testament*, London: Epworth 1953.

Grayston, K. *Dying, We Live: A New Enquiry into the Death of Christ in the New Testament*, London: Darton Longman and Todd 1990.

Griffiths, J. G. *Apuleius of Madauros: The Isis Book*, Leiden: Brill 1975.

Gunther, J. J. *St Paul's Opponents and Their Background: A Study of Apocalyptic and Jewish Sectarian Teaching*, Leiden: Brill 1973.

Hay, D. M. *Glory at the Right Hand: Psalm 110 in Early Christianity*, New York: Abingdon 1973.

Heine, S. *Women and Early Christianity*, London: SCM Press 1987.

Hinson, G. 'The Christian Household in Colossians 3.18–4.1', *Review and Expositor* 70, 1973, 495–506.

Hill, D. *Greek Words and Hebrew Meanings: Studies in the Semantics of Soteriological Terms*, Cambridge University Press 1967.

Hooker, M. D. 'Were There False Teachers in Colossae?' in *Christ and Spirit in the New Testament: Studies in honour of Charles Francis Digby Moule*, ed. B. Lindars and S. S. Smalley, Cambridge University Press 1973, 315–31.

Hooker, M. D., and Wilson, S. G., eds, *Paul and Paulinism: Essays in honour of C. K. Barrett*, London: SPCK 1982.

Hunter, A. M. *Paul and His Predecessors*, London: SCM Press, rev. ed. 1961.

Käsemann, E. 'A Primitive Christian Baptismal Liturgy' in *Essays on New Testament Themes* (SBT 41), London: SCM Press 1964, 149–68.

Kiley, M. *Colossians and Pseudepigraphy*, Sheffield: JSOT Press 1986.

Knox, J. *Philemon Among the Letters of Paul*, London: Collins 1960.

Knox, W. L. *St Paul and the Church of the Gentiles* Cambridge University Press 1938.

Koep, L. *Das himmlische Buch*, Bonn: Hanstein 1952.

Ladd, G. E. 'Paul's Friends in Colossians 4.7–16', *Review and Expositor* 70, 1973, 507–14.

Leaney, A. R. C. 'Colossians 2.21–23 (the use of *pros*)', *ET* 64, 1952–3, 92.

Liddell, H. G., and Scott, R. *A Greek-English Lexicon*, Oxford: Clarendon Press, 9th ed. 1940.

Lincoln, A. T. *Paradise Now and Not Yet: Studies in the Role of the Heavenly Dimension in Paul's Thought With Special Reference to His Eschatology*, Cambridge University Press 1981.

Lofthouse, W. F. 'Singular and Plural in St Paul's Letters', *ET* 58, 1947, 179–82.

Lyonnet, S. 'Paul's Adversaries in Colossae' in Francis and Meeks, *Conflict at Colossae*, 147–61.

Macgregor G. H. C. 'The Concept of the Wrath of God in the New Testament', *NTS* 7, 1960–1961, 101–09.
— 'Principalities and Powers: the Cosmic Background of Paul's Thought', *NTS* 1, 1954, 17–28.
Martin, R. P. *Colossians: The Church's Lord and the Christian's Liberty*, Exeter: Paternoster 1972.
— 'Reconciliation and Forgiveness in the Letter to the Colossians' in R. Banks, *Reconciliation and Hope*, 104–24.
Meeks, W. A. *The First Urban Christians: The Social World of the Apostle Paul*, New Haven: Yale University Press 1983.
McCown, W. 'The Hymnic Structure of Colossians 1.15–20', *EQ* 51, 1979, 156–62.
Metzger, B. M. *The Text of the New Testament*, Oxford: Clarendon Press 1964.
Mitton, C. L. *The Epistle to the Ephesians: Its Authorship, Origin and Purpose*, Oxford: Clarendon Press 1951.
Morrison, C. D. *The Powers That Be* (SBT 29), London: SCM Press 1960.
Moule C. F. D. '"The New Life" in Colossians 3.1–17', *Review and Expositor* 70, 1973, 481–93.
— *The Origin of Christology*, Cambridge University Press 1977.
Moulton, J. H. *A Grammar of New Testament Greek*, Vol. I, *Prolegomena*, Edinburgh: T. and T. Clarke 1906; Vol. III, *Syntax*, by N. Turner, Edinburgh: T. and T. Clarke 1963.
Mullins, T. Y. 'The Thanksgiving in Philemon and Colossians', *NTS* 30, 1984, 228–93.
Norden, E. *Agnostos Theos: Untersuchungen zur Formengeschichte religiöser Rede* Leipzig 1913; 4th ed: Darmstadt: Wissenschaftliche Buchgesellschaft 1956.
O'Brien, P. T. *Introductory Thanksgivings in the Letters of Paul*, (*Nov Test* suppl. 49), Leiden: Brill 1977.
Polehill, J. B. 'The Relationship Between Ephesians and Colossians', *Review and Expositor* 70, 1973, 439–50.
Ramsay, W. M. 'Religious Antiquities of Asia Minor' *ABSA* 18, 1911, 44ff.
— *The Teaching of Paul in Terms of the Present Day*, London, Hodder and Stoughton 1913.
Robinson, J. A. *St Paul's Epistle to the Ephesians*, London: Macmillan 2nd ed. 1904
Robinson, J. A. T. *The Body* (SBT 5), London: SCM Press 1952.

Robinson, J. M. 'A Formal Analysis of Colossians 1.15–20', *JBL* 76, 1957, 270–87.

Rodd, C. S. 'Salvation Proclaimed: XI Colossians 2.8–15', *ET* 94, 1982–3, 36–41.

Rowland, C. *The Open Heaven: A Study of Apocalyptic Judaism and Early Christianity*. London: SPCK 1982.

— 'Apocalyptic Visions and The Exaltation of Christ in the Letter to the Colossians', *JSNT* 19, 1983, 73–83.

Rudolph, K. *Gnosis: The Nature and History of an Ancient Religion*, Edinburgh: T. and T. Clark 1983.

Sanders, E. P. 'Literary Dependence in Colossians', *JBL* 85, 1966, 28–45.

Sappington, T. J *Revelation and Redemption at Colossae* (JSNTS 53), Sheffield: JSOT Press 1991.

Scholem, G. *Jewish Gnosticism, Merkabah Mysticism and Talmudic Tradition*, New York: The Jewish Theological Seminary of America, 2nd ed. 1965.

—*Major Trends in Jewish Mysticism*, New York, Schocken Books, 3rd ed. 1954.

Schubert, P. *Form and Function of the Pauline Thanksgiving* (BZNW 20), Berlin: Töpelmann, 1939.

Schütz, J. H. *Paul and the Anatomy of Apostolic Authority*, Cambridge University Press 1975

Schweitzer, A. *The Mysticism of Paul the Apostle*, ET London: A. and C. Black 1931.

Selwyn, E. G. *The First Epistle of Peter*, London: Macmillan, 2nd ed. 1947.

Stambaugh, J., and Balch, D. *The Social World of the First Christians*, London: SPCK 1986.

Steindorff, G. *Die Apokalypse des Elias, eine unbekannte Apokalypse, und Bruchstücke der Sophanias-Apokalypse* (TU 17), Leipzig 1899.

Strugnell, J. 'The Angelic Liturgy at Qumran, 4Q *Serek Sirot Olat Hassabbat*', *Congress Volume, Oxford 1959* (*VT* suppl. 7), Leiden: Brill 1960, 318–45.

Tannehill, R. C. *Dying and Rising with Christ*, Berlin: Töpelmann, 1966.

Theissen, G. *The Social Setting of Pauline Christianity*, Edinburgh: T. and T. Clark 1982.

Turner, N. *Grammatical Insights into the New Testament*, Edinburgh: T. and T. Clark 1965.

— *Christian Words*, Edinburgh: T. and T. Clark 1980.

Van der Horst P. W. 'Observations on a Pauline Expressions', *NTS* 19, 1973, 181–7.
Versnel, H. S. *Triumphus. An Inquiry into the Origins, Development and Meaning of the Roman Triumph*, Leiden: Brill, 1970.
Vögtle A. *Die Tugend- und Lastercataloge im Neuen Testament*, Münster: Aschendorff 1936.
Wedderburn, A. J. M. *Baptism and Resurrection: Studies in Pauline Theology Against Its Graeco-Roman Background*, Tübingen: Mohr 1987.
Weidinger, K. *Die Haustafeln: Ein Stück urchristlicher Paranese*, Leipzig: Hinrichs 1928.
Weiss, H. 'The Law in the Epistle to the Colossians', *CBQ* 34, 1972, 294–314.
Wink, W. *Unmasking The Powers: The Invisible Powers That Determine Human Existence*, Philadelphia: Fortress 1986.
Williamson, L. 'Led in Triumph: Paul's Use of Thriambeuō', *Interpretation* 22, 1968, 317–32.
Yates, R. 'A Note on Colossians 1.24', *EQ* 42, 1970, 88–92.
— 'Satan and the Failure of Nerve', *New Blackfriars* 52, 1971, 223–8.
— 'Christ and the Powers of Evil in Colossians', *Studia Biblica 1978* (JSNTS 3), Sheffield: JSOT Press 1980, 461–8.
—'Paul's Affliction in Asia: II Corinthians 1.8', *EQ* 53, 1981, 241–5.
— 'St Paul and the Law in Galatians', *ITQ* 52, 1985, 105–24.
— 'The Worship of Angels (Col. 2.18)', *ET* 97, 1985, 12–15.
— 'Colossians and Gnosis', *JSNT* 27, 1986, 49–68.
— 'Colossians 2.14: Metaphor of Forgiveness', *Biblica* 71, 1990, 248–59.
— 'The Christian Way of Life: The Paraentic Material in Colossians 3.1–4.6', *EQ* 63, 1991, 241–52.
— 'Colossians 2.15: Christ Triumphant', *NTS* 37, 1991, 573–91.
— 'A Re-Appraisal of Colossians', *ITQ* 58, 1992, 95–117.
Ziesler J. *Paul's Letter to the Romans*, London: SCM Press 1989.
—*Pauline Christianity*, Oxford University Press 1983.